APPALACHIAN TRAIL

Data Book

2021

Forty-third Edition

Daniel D. Chazin, *Editor*

Harpers Ferry

Cover photograph: Below Avery Peak in Maine © Kenneth J. Sgorbati

Forty-third edition
First published in 1977

Printed in the United States

ISBN 978-1-944958-16-9

APPALACHIAN TRAIL

Data Book

2021

Contents

Notice to All Trail Users

The information in this publication is the result of the best effort of the publisher, using data available to it at the time of printing. Changes resulting from maintenance work and relocations are constantly occurring and, therefore, no published route can be regarded as precisely accurate at the time you read this notice.

Notices of pending relocations are indicated in current Appalachian Trail guidebooks, whenever possible.

Because maintenance of the Trail is conducted by volunteers and maintaining clubs listed in the appropriate guidebooks, questions about the exact route of the Trail should be addressed to the maintaining clubs or the Appalachian Trail Conservancy, P.O. Box 807, Harpers Ferry, WV 25425 (telephone: 304-535-6331; e-mail: <info@appalachiantrail.org>). On the Trail, please pay close attention to — and follow — the white blazes and any directional signs.

There are few things more rewarding than hiking the Appalachian Trail, whether you come to it as a novice looking to spend only a couple of hours outdoors or a Trail-tested veteran who has thru-hiked more than once.

Regardless of your skill, it is extremely important to plan your hike, especially in places where water is scarce. Purify water drawn from any source. Water purity cannot be guaranteed. The Appalachian Trail Conservancy and the various maintaining clubs attempt to locate good sources of water along the Trail but have no control over those sources and cannot, in any sense, be responsible for the quality of the water at any given time. You should ensure the safety of all water you use by treating it.

Certain risks are inherent in any Appalachian Trail hike. Each A.T. user must accept personal responsibility for his or her safety while on the Trail. The Appalachian Trail Conservancy and its member maintaining clubs cannot ensure the safety of any hiker on the Trail, and, when undertaking a hike on the Trail, each user thereby assumes the risk for any accident, illness, or injury that might occur on the Trail.

Enjoy your hike, but please take all appropriate precautions for your safety and well-being.

Safety and Ethics

Although the Appalachian Trail is safer than most places, you should be aware that problems do occur, and a few crimes of violence have occurred during the past four decades. Safety, or situational, awareness is one of your best lines of defense. Be aware of what you are doing, where you are, and to whom you are talking. Here are some suggestions:

- *Use extra caution if hiking alone.* If you are by yourself and encounter a stranger who makes you feel uncomfortable, say you are with a group that is behind you. Be creative. If in doubt, move on.
- *Leave your hiking itinerary and timetable* with someone at home. Be sure he or she knows your Trail name, if you have one. Check in regularly, and establish a procedure to follow if you fail to check in. It helps to let ATC know your name and Trail name, in case a family member needs to reach you during an extended hike. However, *do not broadcast your itinerary or location in real time* on on-line journals or blogs.
- *Be wary of strangers.* Be friendly, but cautious. Don't tell strangers your plans. Avoid people who act suspiciously, hostile, or intoxicated.
- *Don't camp near road crossings.*
- *Carrying firearms is discouraged.* Although it is now legal to carry (but not discharge) on National Park Service lands and in most other areas, with the proper state-by-state permits, they could be turned against you, you face a high risk of an accidental shooting, and they are extra weight, observe many veteran A.T. hikers.
- *Eliminate opportunities for theft.* Don't bring jewelry. Hide your money. If you must leave your pack, hide it carefully, or leave it with someone trustworthy. Don't leave valuables or equipment (especially in sight) in vehicles parked at Trailheads.
- *Use the Trail and shelter registers.* Sign in, leave a note, and report any suspicious activities. If someone needs to locate you, or if a serious

crime has been committed along the Trail, the first place authorities will look is in the registers.

- *Report any crime or harassment* to the local law-enforcement authorities *and* ask them to contact the National Park Service 24-hour communications center at (866) 677-6677. See below for emergencies when you need immediate response. You can also let ATC know by sending an e-mail to <incident@appalachiantrail.org> or calling the information desk at (304) 535-6331. Facebook ***is not*** "911."

As the A.T. becomes increasingly used, the potential for problems could increase. Help to keep the Trail a safe place. Maintain your safety awareness, help each other, and report all incidents. *More detailed advice is available at <www.appalachiantrail.org/explore/plan-and-prepare/hiking-basics/safety/>.* Be prudent and cautious without allowing common sense to slip into paranoia. Trust your gut.

Reporting Trail Emergencies

Check the map, guidebook, nearest shelter, or Trailhead facility for local emergency telephone numbers. Leave the Trail at the nearest road crossing, and find a telephone or cellular-phone reception. Know your location and the location of the incident as precisely as possible. Dial "911" or "0" (ask the operator to connect you with the nearest state-police facility), and make your report. Ask the dispatcher to contact the National Park Service 24-hour communications center at (866) 677-6677.

Public Transportation

The Appalachian Trail Conservancy maintains information on public transportation to the Trail on its Web site at *<www.appalachiantrail.org/home/explore-the-trail/transportation-options>*.

Coronavirus

The coronavirus pandemic is expected to remain a concern throughout the 2021 hiking season, and some shelters may be closed. For periodic updates and advice, please check the ATC Web site at <appalachiantrail.org/official-blog/a-reminder-to-stay-safe-on-the-at/>.

Leave No Trace®

The Appalachian Trail Conservancy, in partnership with the Leave No Trace Center for Outdoor Ethics, asks you to help take care of the Appalachian Trail and the wild country it passes through. Please do your part by following the seven Leave No Trace principles of low-impact use while in the backcountry:

1. Plan ahead and prepare.
2. Travel and camp on durable surfaces.
3. Dispose of waste properly.
4. Leave what you find.
5. Minimize campfire impacts.
6. Respect wildlife.
7. Be considerate of other visitors.

More specific ways those principles apply to the Appalachian Trail can be found at <www.appalachiantrail.org/Lnt>. The continued existence of the Trail depends, in part, on proper use by those who walk on it. Particular care should be taken not to damage the footpath itself, natural features alongside it, or the property of others, through littering or other vandalism, improper fires, or use of vehicles. The needs of other users should always be considered, and special regulations must be followed in many areas. Please keep day-hiking groups to 25 people or fewer and overnight groups to no more than 10 people.

Although more than 99 percent of the Appalachian Trail now crosses public land, the remainder is on private or municipal property, thanks to the cooperation and good faith of the landowners. The Conservancy and its member clubs strongly urge all users of the Trail to respect those private lands and the owners' rights as if the lands were their own.

Public lands are, in a sense, the user's own—shared with all other users—so please proceed accordingly, taking care to obey any regulations imposed on use of the Trail in a particular section. **For example, camping permits are required before entering Great Smoky Mountains National Park.** On many other parts of the Trail, camping is permitted only in designated areas.

Again, please consult the guidebooks and maps, and watch for special signs along the Trail.

And, enjoy your hike!

Useful Features of the *A.T. Data Book*

This publication provides a ready reference for hikers to the major features of the Appalachian Trail as it winds for more than 2,190 miles from Maine to Georgia. Many hikers find it indispensable to their journeys on the A.T. and save each year's edition with a record of their experiences and accomplishments.

The features listed here include shelters and campsites, road crossings, sources of water, elevations, principal mountain peaks and gaps, and other notable physical landmarks of America's foremost national scenic trail. Locations of areas where lodging, meals, groceries, and post offices are available also are listed, with distances and directions. Additionally, each section is marked with the Trail-maintaining club associated with that segment, and Web-site information for the clubs may be found on page 85.

The *Data Book* is intended to be useful in broad-scale planning of a trip of any length on the Trail, from home or while on the footpath itself.

The *Data Book* does not, however, include sufficient detail for careful, complete planning of a trip. Potential hikers are encouraged to purchase separately the official *Appalachian Trail Guide* book-and-maps set for the state(s) they plan to hike (not to be confused with the *A.T. Guide* thru-hiking book from a commercial publisher). The guidebooks contain detailed descriptions of Trail sections, facilities near the Trail, points of interest off the Trail, background on the history and natural features of the area, and other important information.

All guidebooks are sold with sets of maps for the state(s) described, another key to a safe and enjoyable hike. Guidebooks, maps, and other ATC publications may be ordered by visiting Mountaineers Books *via* <*www.mountaineersbooks.org*>, or calling (206) 223-6303.

The compilation of each edition of the *Data Book* begins with the latest *Appalachian Trail Guides*. The distances and descriptive information are updated to take into account relocations since the last edition.

This information is supplied to the Conservancy by its member clubs and volunteers who help ensure access to the Appalachian Trail experience for all. Each year, more than 6,000 volunteers contribute more than 200,000 hours of work to various projects along the Trail.

The data has been cross-checked by both volunteers and staff members. However, it is impossible to ensure absolute accuracy of the information, and changes may occur during the year of this edition. Trail-enhancing relocations that affect distances between major features are underway in some states. Also, severe weather conditions, fires, and other unpredictable developments might force temporary closings of a section.

Users of the Trail for any period of time should carefully follow the painted white blazes and signs that mark the current route of the Trail.

Hikers finding errors or omissions in the *Data Book* are urged to report them, by e-mail to <publisher@appalachiantrail.org>, or by mail to Data Book Editor, Appalachian Trail Conservancy, P.O. Box 807, Harpers Ferry, WV 25425. Confirmed changes will be included in the next edition.

How to Use the *Data Book*

The *Data Book* is divided into twelve chapters, beginning with Maine (at Katahdin) and ending with the Approach Trail to Springer Mountain in Georgia. With one exception, each chapter corresponds to a volume in the current series of *Appalachian Trail Guides* (see page 4 for ordering information). The section beginning on page 27, for example, matches the third volume in the guidebook series, which covers the Trail in Massachusetts–Connecticut. The exception is the Trail route through the Great Smokies of Tennessee and North Carolina, which is covered in both the Tennessee–North Carolina and North Carolina–Georgia guidebooks. It is included here only in Chapter Ten (Tennessee–North Carolina).

Georgia A.T. Club

Trail-maintaining clubs are listed in the outside margins next to the section(s) of Trail that each club maintains. The beginning and ending points of each club's range are indicated by a small gray rectangle. Web site information for the clubs may be found on page 85.

N.C. Section 11

Trail sections, as numbered and identified in the corresponding guide, are given in the columns to the left on each page, under the heading *GBS* (guidebook section). Sections are numbered consecutively, from north to south, within each state.

In the right column, under the heading *Map*, the number of the map that covers the area is given. For more detail about a particular feature or section of the Trail, consult the relevant guidebook section or map.

Each section contains a list of features along or near the Trail.

Towns with post offices (P.O.) are printed in boldface and carry their ZIP Code in the listing. Towns without post offices are listed only if the Trail goes directly through them; "P.O." is omitted in those cases.

Greenwood Lake, N.Y., P.O. 10925

The *elevations* of selected points along the Trail follow the name of the feature. Those elevations are intended to represent the most significant points in terms of elevation gain and loss and provide the hiker with a general sense of the elevation change along each section of the hike. Of course, many ups and downs have not been referenced in this book, and the difficulty of the terrain may vary considerably. Hikers should use the elevations provided only as a general guide.

Rainbow Ledges (1,517')

In general, all *facilities* within five miles of the Trail by road are included, unless similar facilities are located closer to the footpath or a facility's inclusion would not significantly benefit the hiker. In some cases, where a particular facility is not available for a great distance, we have included facilities that are more than five miles from the Trail but still within 12 miles.

To the right of the list of features, facilities, if any, are noted with a one-letter code. The codes are explained on pages 8–9.

Low Gap Cw

Except for shelters, campsites, and water sources located on the Trail itself—or within 0.1 mile of the footpath—the listing for a facility includes the distance and direction to it. So, if the symbols "C", "S", or "w" appear without direction and distance information in the listing, that campsite, shelter, or water source is on the Trail or within about 500 feet of it.

The number to the left of a feature is the *distance* — in miles — of the feature from the northern end of the part of the Trail covered in that particular chapter (read down). The number to the right of the features and facilities lists, correspondingly, is the feature's distance from the southern end of the part of the Trail covered by this chapter (read up). The starting point for the cumulative distance is given at the top of the column.

Miles from Katahdin			*Miles from Maine–N.H. Line*
0.0	Katahdin (Baxter Peak) (5,268')		281.8
1.0	Thoreau Spring	w	280.8

Sometimes the Trail follows a road, ridge line, lake, creek, or other physical feature for some distance. In those cases, usually only one distance is listed. For roads, this is generally the point at which the Trail first reaches the road proceeding from north to south, or, in some cases, the point representing the end of the section. For ridge lines, this is the highest point. Again, for more complete information about a particular feature, please consult the guidebooks, maps, or both.

Codes

C *Campsites and campgrounds.* For New Hampshire, the "C" code is also used to indicate those shelters at which tent camping also is permitted.

E *"East,"* used to designate direction to facilities that are to the right of the Trail when traveling north (*i.e.*, toward Katahdin).

G *Groceries, supplies.*

L *Lodgings other than Trail shelters, campsites, and campgrounds:* for example, motels, hotels, cottages, and hostels. This code is also used for the Appalachian Mountain Club (AMC) huts in New Hampshire and camps (commercial cottages) in Maine.

m *Miles.*

M *Meals; restaurants.*

nw *No potable water.* This is used in shelter and campsite listings only.

P.O. *Post office.* Towns without post offices are listed only if the Trail goes directly through them; "P.O." is omitted in those cases.

R *Road access.* Only roads open to the public and passable by ordinary automobiles are designated. Included are road crossings and locations where the Trail runs along a road or is adjacent to a road that provides access to the Trail. Where the road crossings are frequent (every two miles or less), lesser ones are omitted.

S *Shelter.* A three-sided structure, with or without bunks or floors, intended as overnight housing for hikers (also known as lean-tos in some areas). Included in this category are unlocked cabins or lodges, found primarily in New Hampshire, Vermont, Pennsylvania, and Maryland. (See also "L".)

W *"West,"* used to designate direction to facilities that are to the left of the Trail when traveling north (*i.e.,* toward Katahdin).

w *Water* (from springs, streams, *etc.*). In general, where available, water sources are listed about every three to four miles. Other water sources do exist, and not every water source is listed in the *Data Book*. ***Note: All water should be purified before use.***

☆ Indicates an **Appalachian Trail Community**, a town designated by the ATC as a participant in A.T. protection work through local education initiatives and land-conservation activity, while ATC helps it with "green tourism" development. A list of designated towns and counties can be found on page 87.

Appalachian Trail Distances

These sections and Trail points correspond to the beginnings and endings of chapters in this book and the eleven-volume series of official Appalachian Trail Guides.

Length by Section

Section	Miles
Maine	281.8
New Hampshire–Vermont	311.7
Massachusetts–Connecticut	140.9
New York–New Jersey	162.4
Pennsylvania	229.3
Maryland–West Virginia–Northern Virginia	94.9
Shenandoah National Park	107.8
Central Virginia	226.8
Southwest Virginia	166.8
Tennessee–North Carolina	304.0
North Carolina–Georgia	166.7

Cumulative Distances

Miles from Katahdin		*Miles from Springer Mountain*
0.0	Baxter Peak, Katahdin, Maine	2,193.1
281.8	Maine–New Hampshire Line	1,911.3
593.5	Vermont–Massachusetts Line	1,599.6
734.4	Connecticut–New York Line	1,458.7
896.8	New Jersey–Pennsylvania Line	1,296.3
1,126.1	Pennsylvania–Maryland Line	1,067.0
1,221.0	Front Royal, Virginia	972.1
1,328.8	Rockfish Gap, Virginia	864.3
1,555.6	New River, Virginia	637.5
1,722.4	Damascus, Virginia	470.7
2,026.4	Fontana Dam, North Carolina	166.7
2,193.1	Springer Mountain, Georgia	0.0

Maine

GBS	N to S	Features	Facilities (see page 8 for codes)	S to N	Map
	Miles from Katahdin			*Miles from Maine–N.H. Line*	
Maine Section 1	0.0	Katahdin (Baxter Peak) (5,268')		281.8	*Maine A.T. Club*; Maine Map 1
	1.0	Thoreau Spring	w	280.8	
	4.0	Katahdin Stream Falls	w	277.8	
	5.2	Katahdin Stream Campground, Birches Campsite (1,070') (C,S,w on A.T.)	CSw	276.6	
	5.3	Cross Tote Road	R	276.5	
	7.5	Daicey Pond Campground Road (L,w 0.1m E)	RLw	274.3	
	8.8	Big Niagara Falls	w	273.0	
	9.6	Upper Fork Nesowadnehunk Stream (ford)	w	272.2	
	10.5	Lower Fork Nesowadnehunk Stream (ford)	w	271.3	
	11.0	Pine Point	w	270.8	
	14.0	Katahdin Stream	w	267.8	
	14.4	Abol Stream, Baxter Park Boundary		267.4	
Maine Section 2	15.1	Abol Bridge over West Branch of Penobscot River; junction with International A.T. (588') (C,G,w on A.T.)	RCGw	266.7	
	18.6	Hurd Brook Lean-to (710')	Sw	263.2	
	21.1	Rainbow Ledges (1,517')		260.7	
	22.9	Rainbow Lake (east end)	w	258.9	
	26.3	Rainbow Spring Campsite	Cw	255.5	
	28.1	Rainbow Lake (west end) Side Trail	w	253.7	
	30.1	Rainbow Stream Lean-to (1,020')	Sw	251.7	
	32.5	Pollywog Stream (682')	w	249.3	
	33.9	Crescent Pond (west end)	w	247.9	
	36.3	Nesuntabunt Mountain (1,520')		245.5	
	38.2	Wadleigh Stream Lean-to	Sw	243.6	
	40.8	Nahmakanta Lake (south end) (650')	Rw	241.0	

Maine

GBS	N to S	Features	Facilities (see page 8 for codes)	S to N	Map
	Miles from Katahdin			*Miles from Maine–N.H. Line*	
Maine A.T. Club / Maine Section 3	42.5	Tumbledown Dick Trail		239.3	Maine Map 2
	44.0	Nahmakanta Stream Lean-to	Sw	237.8	
	46.0	Logging Road	R		
		(C,L,M 1m E)	RCLM	235.8	
	47.7	Pemadumcook Lake (southwest shore)	w	234.1	
	48.3	Potaywadjo Spring Lean-to (710')	Sw	233.5	
	50.1	Sand Beach, Lower Jo-Mary Lake	w	231.7	
	51.8	Antlers Campsite (500')	Cw	230.0	
	53.1	Mud Pond (outlet)	w	228.7	
	56.0	Jo-Mary Road			
		(w on A.T.; C,G 6m E)	RCGw	225.8	
	59.7	Cooper Brook Falls Lean-to (880')	Sw	222.1	
	62.0	Crawford Pond (outlet)	w	219.8	
	62.9	Kokadjo–B Pond Road	R	218.9	
	64.3	Little Boardman Mountain (1,980')		217.5	
	65.6	Spring	w	216.2	
	65.9	Mountain View Pond (outlet)	w	215.9	
	67.5	East Branch of Pleasant River (ford)	w	214.3	
	67.8	East Branch Lean-to (1,225')	Sw	214.0	
	69.8	West Branch Ponds Road			
		(L,M 4m W)	RLM	212.0	
	71.4	Logan Brook Lean-to (2,480')	Sw	210.4	
	72.8	White Cap Mountain (3,650')		209.0	
	73.9	White Brook Trail		207.9	
	74.5	Hay Mountain		207.3	
	76.1	West Peak		205.7	
	76.8	Sidney Tappan Campsite (2,425')	Cw	205.0	
	77.7	Gulf Hagas Mountain		204.1	
	78.6	Carl A. Newhall Lean-to (1,860')	Sw	203.2	
	82.1	Gulf Hagas Cut-off Trail	w	199.7	

Maine

GBS	N to S	Features	Facilities (see page 8 for codes)	S to N	Map
	Miles from Katahdin			*Miles from Maine–N.H. Line*	
Maine 3	82.8	Gulf Hagas Trail	w	199.0	Map 2
	83.8	The Hermitage (695') (C,w 0.7m E)	Cw	198.0	
Maine Section 4	84.1	West Branch of Pleasant River (ford)	w	197.7	Maine Map 3 *Maine A.T. Club*
	84.6	Katahdin Iron Works Road	R	197.2	
	85.8	East Chairback Pond Side Trail (1,630') (w 0.2m W)	w	196.0	
	88.0	Chairback Mountain (2,180')		193.8	
	88.5	Chairback Gap Lean-to (1,930')	Sw	193.3	
	88.9	Columbus Mountain (2,325')		192.9	
	90.2	West Chairback Pond Side Trail (1,770')	w	191.6	
	90.8	Third Mountain, Monument Cliff (1,920')		191.0	
	93.3	Fourth Mountain (2,380')		188.5	
	95.4	Cloud Pond Lean-to Side Trail (S,w 0.3m E)	Sw	186.4	
	96.3	Barren Mountain (2,660')		185.5	
	99.4	Long Pond Stream Lean-to (940')	Sw	182.4	
	100.2	Long Pond Stream (ford) (620')	w	181.6	
	104.1	Wilson Valley Lean-to (1,045')	Sw	177.7	
	104.5	Central Maine & Quebec Railway		177.3	
	104.8	Big Wilson Stream (ford) (600')	w	177.0	
	107.7	Little Wilson Stream	w	174.1	
	107.9	Little Wilson Falls		173.9	
	110.7	North Pond (outlet)	w	171.1	
	111.5	Leeman Brook Lean-to (1,060')	Sw	170.3	
	112.6	Lily Pond	w	169.2	
	113.3	Bell Pond	w	168.5	
	114.4	Spectacle Pond (outlet)	w	167.4	
	114.5	Maine 15 (1,215')	R	167.3	

Maine

GBS	N to S	Features	Facilities (see page 8 for codes)	S to N	Map
	Miles from Katahdin			*Miles from Maine–N.H. Line*	
Maine Section 5	117.8	**Monson, Maine, P.O. 04464** (900')	☆		Maine Map 4
		(P.O.,C,G,L,M 2m E)	CGLM	164.0	
	120.8	Shirley–Blanchard Road	R	161.0	
	121.2	East Branch of Piscataquis River (ford)	w	160.6	
	123.5	Horseshoe Canyon Lean-to (870')	Sw	158.3	
	126.6	West Branch of Piscataquis River (ford)	w	155.2	
	130.3	Bald Mountain Pond (outlet)	w	151.5	
	132.4	Moxie Bald Lean-to (1,220')	Sw	149.4	
	134.5	Moxie Bald Mountain (2,629')		147.3	
	136.5	Bald Mountain Brook Lean-to (1,300')	Sw	145.3	
	139.3	Moxie Pond (south end) (970')	Rw	142.5	
	144.2	Pleasant Pond Mountain (2,470')		137.6	
	145.5	Pleasant Pond Lean-to (1,320')	Sw	136.3	
	145.9	Boise-Cascade Logging Road	R	135.9	
	148.5	Holly Brook	w	133.3	
	151.2	U.S. 201; **Caratunk, Maine, P.O. 04925**			
		(P.O. 0.3m E; C,L,M 2m W)	RCLM	130.6	
Maine Section 6	151.5	Kennebec River (490')	w	130.3	
	154.8	Trail to Harrison's Pierce Pond Camps			
		(L,M 0.3m E; w 0.1m E)	RLMw	127.0	
	155.2	Pierce Pond Lean-to (1,160')	Sw	126.6	Maine Map 5
	158.7	North Branch of Carrying Place Stream	w	123.1	
	159.4	Logging Road	R	122.4	
	161.1	East Carry Pond (north end)	w	120.7	
	162.6	Sandy Stream, Middle Carry Pond (inlet)	w	119.2	
	164.5	West Carry Pond (east side)	w	117.3	
	165.2	West Carry Pond Lean-to (1,340')	Sw	116.6	
	165.9	West Carry Pond (west side)	w	115.9	
	167.0	Roundtop Mountain (1,760')		114.8	
	168.7	Long Falls Dam Road (1,225')	R	113.1	

Maine A.T. Club

Maine

GBS	N to S	Features	Facilities (see page 8 for codes)	S to N	Map
	Miles from Katahdin			*Miles from Maine–N.H. Line*	
Maine Section 7	170.4	Campsite	Cw	111.4	Maine Map 5
	171.4	Bog Brook Road, Flagstaff Lake (inlet)	Rw	110.4	
	171.5	East Flagstaff Road	R	110.3	
	172.9	Little Bigelow Lean-to (1,760')	Sw	108.9	
	174.6	Little Bigelow Mountain (east end) (3,010')		107.2	
	177.8	Safford Notch Campsite (2,230') (C,w 0.3m E)	Cw	104.0	
	177.9	Safford Brook Trail		103.9	
	179.8	Bigelow Mountain (Avery Peak) (4,090')		102.0	
	180.2	Avery Memorial Campsite, Bigelow Col, Fire Warden's Trail	Cw	101.6	
	180.5	Bigelow Mountain (West Peak) (4,145')		101.3	
	182.6	South Horn		99.2	
	183.1	Horns Pond Lean-tos (3,160')	CSw	98.7	
	183.3	Horns Pond Trail		98.5	
	185.0	Bigelow Range Trail, Cranberry Pond (w 0.2m W)	w	96.8	
	186.3	Cranberry Stream Campsite (1,350')	Cw	95.5	
	187.2	Stratton Brook (1,230')	w	94.6	
	187.4	Stratton Brook Pond Road	R	94.4	
Maine Section 8	188.2	Maine 27; **Stratton, Maine, P.O. 04982** (P.O.,G,L,M 5m W)	RGLM	93.6	
	193.4	North Crocker Mountain (4,228')		88.4	Maine Map 6
	194.4	South Crocker Mountain (4,040')		87.4	
	195.5	Crocker Cirque Campsite Side Trail (2,710') (w on A.T.; C 0.2m E)	Cw	86.3	
	196.5	Caribou Valley Road (2,220')		85.3	
	196.6	South Branch Carrabassett River (ford)	w	85.2	
	198.8	Sugarloaf Mountain Trail		83.0	
	200.9	Spaulding Mountain (4,000')		80.9	

Maine A.T. Club

Maine

GBS	N to S	Features	Facilities (see page 8 for codes)	S to N	Map
	Miles from Katahdin			*Miles from Maine–N.H. Line*	
Maine Section 8	201.7	Spaulding Mountain Lean-to (3,140')	Sw	80.1	Maine Map 6
	202.8	Mt. Abraham Trail		79.0	
	203.9	Lone Mountain (3,260')		77.9	
	207.0	Orbeton Stream (ford) (1,550')	w	74.8	
	209.7	Poplar Ridge Lean-to (2,960')	Sw	72.1	
	210.7	Stream	w	71.1	
	211.1	Saddleback Junior (3,655')		70.7	
	212.4	Redington Stream Campsite	Cw	69.4	
	213.1	The Horn (4,040')		68.7	
	214.7	Saddleback Mountain (4,120')		67.1	
	216.7	Eddy Pond	w	65.1	
	218.6	Piazza Rock Lean-to (2,065')	Sw	63.2	
	220.3	Sandy River (1,595')	w	61.5	
Maine Section 9	220.4	Maine 4; **Rangeley, Maine, P.O. 04970** (P.O.,C,G,L,M 9m W)	☆ RCGLM	61.4	
	222.5	South Pond (2,174')	w	59.3	
	225.2	Little Swift River Pond Campsite (2,460')	Cw	56.6	
	229.8	Sabbath Day Pond Lean-to	Sw	52.0	
	230.1	Long Pond (2,330')	w	51.7	
	231.9	Moxie Pond	w	49.9	
	233.5	Maine 17; **Oquossoc, Maine, P.O. 04964** (P.O.,G,L,M 11m W)	RGLM	48.3	
Maine 10	234.3	Bemis Stream (ford) (1,495')	w	47.5	Maine Map 7
	238.1	Bemis Mountain Lean-to (2,800')	Sw	43.7	
	239.8	Bemis Range (West Peak) (3,580')		42.0	
	240.8	Bemis Stream Trail		41.0	
	244.0	Old Blue Mountain (3,600')		37.8	
Maine 11	246.8	South Arm Road, Black Brook (ford) (1,410') (C,w on A.T.; C,G 4.5m W)	RCGw	35.0	
	248.6	Moody Mountain (2,440)		33.2	

Maine A.T. Club

Maine

GBS	N to S	Features	Facilities (see page 8 for codes)	S to N	Map
	Miles from Katahdin			*Miles from Maine–N.H. Line*	
Maine 11	249.5	Sawyer Notch, Sawyer Brook (ford) (1,095')	w	32.3	Maine Map 7 / *Maine Appalachian Trail Club*
	250.9	Hall Mountain Lean-to (2,650')	Sw	30.9	
	252.2	Wyman Mountain (2,920')		29.6	
	255.1	Surplus Pond (outlet)	w	26.7	
Maine Section 12	256.9	East B Hill Road (1,485'); **Andover, Maine, P.O. 04216** (P.O.,C,G,L,M 8m E)	RCGLM	24.9	
	257.7	Dunn Notch and Falls	w	24.1	
	261.4	Frye Notch Lean-to (2,280')	Sw	20.4	
	263.2	Baldpate Mountain (East Peak), Grafton Loop Trail (3,810')		18.6	
	264.1	Baldpate Mountain (West Peak) (3,662')		17.7	
	264.9	Baldpate Lean-to (2,660')	Sw	16.9	
Maine Section 13	267.2	Grafton Notch, Maine 26 (1,495')	R	14.6	*Appalachian Mountain Club*
	268.3	Brook	w	13.5	
	270.7	Old Speck Trail, Grafton Loop Trail (3,985')		11.1	
	271.8	Speck Pond Shelter and Campsite, Speck Pond Trail	CSw	10.0	
	272.7	Mahoosuc Arm (3,770')		9.1	
	274.3	Mahoosuc Notch (east end) (2,150')	w	7.5	
	275.4	Mahoosuc Notch (west end), Mahoosuc Notch Trail	w	6.4	
	276.4	Fulling Mill Mountain (South Peak) (3,395')		5.4	
	276.9	Full Goose Shelter and Campsite	CSw	4.9	
	277.9	Goose Eye Mountain (North Peak)		3.9	
	279.1	Goose Eye Mountain (East Peak) (3,790')		2.7	
	280.9	Mt. Carlo (3,565')		0.9	
	281.3	Carlo Col Trail, Carlo Col Shelter and Campsite (C,S,w 0.3m W)	CSw	0.5	
	281.8	Maine–New Hampshire Line (2,972')		0.0	

New Hampshire–Vermont

GBS	N to S	Features	Facilities (see page 8 for codes)	S to N	Map
	Miles from Maine–N.H. Line			*Miles from Vt.–Mass. Line*	
N.H Section 1	0.0	Maine–New Hampshire Line (2,972')		311.7	N.H.–Vt. Map 1
	1.9	Mt. Success (3,565')		309.8	
	4.7	Gentian Pond Shelter/Campsite (2,166')	CSw	307.0	
	5.4	Moss Pond	w	306.3	
	6.9	Dream Lake	w	304.8	
	9.6	Trident Col Tentsite (2,020')	Cw	302.1	
	10.7	Cascade Mountain (2,631')		301.0	
	15.0	Brook	w	296.7	
	16.2	Androscoggin River (750')	R	295.5	
N.H. Section 2	16.5	U.S. 2; **Gorham, N.H., P.O. 03581** ☆ (w on A.T.; P.O.,G,L,M 3.6m W; C,L,M 1.8m W)	RCGLMw	295.2	
	18.4	Rattle River Shelter	Sw	293.3	N.H.–Vt. Map 2
	22.4	Mt. Moriah (4,049')		289.3	
	24.5	Imp Shelter/Campsite (3,250')	CSw	287.2	
	27.0	Middle Carter Mountain (4,610')		284.7	
	29.1	Zeta Pass (3,890')		282.6	
	30.5	Carter Dome (4,832')		281.2	
	31.0	Spring	w	280.7	
	31.7	Carter Notch, Carter Notch Hut (3,350') (L,M,w 0.2m E)	LMw	280.0	
	32.6	Wildcat Mountain, Peak A (4,422')		279.1	
	34.6	Wildcat Mountain, Peak D		277.1	
N.H. Section 3	37.6	Pinkham Notch, N.H. 16, Pinkham Notch Camp (2,050') (L,M,w on A.T.)	RLMw	274.1	
	39.7	Lowe's Bald Spot (2,860')		272.0	
	41.6	West Branch, Peabody River (2,300')	w	270.1	
	42.4	Osgood Tentsite	Cw	269.3	
	44.9	Mt. Madison (5,366')		266.8	

Appalachian Mountain Club

New Hampshire–Vermont

GBS	N to S	Features	Facilities (see page 8 for codes)	S to N	Map
	Miles from Maine–N.H. Line			*Miles from Vt.–Mass. Line*	
N.H. Section 3	45.4	Madison Spring Hut, Valley Way Tentsite (C,w 0.6m W; L,M,w on A.T.)	CLMw	266.3	N.H.–Vt. Map 2; *Randolph Mountain Club*
	46.3	Thunderstorm Junction, Spur Trail to Crag Camp Cabin, Lowe's Path to Mt. Adams & Gray Knob Cabin (S,w 1.1m W, 1.2m W)	Sw	265.4	
	46.9	Israel Ridge Path to The Perch Shelter (C,S,w 0.9m W)	CSw	264.8	
	47.6	Edmands Col (4,938')		264.1	*Appalachian Mountain Club*
	51.1	**Mt. Washington, N.H., P.O. 03589** (6,288') (P.O.,M on A.T.)	RM	260.6	
	52.5	Lakes of the Clouds Hut (5,012') (L,M,w on A.T.)	LMw	259.2	
	53.6	Mt. Franklin		258.1	
	54.2	Spring	w	257.5	
	55.5	Spring	w	256.2	
	56.4	Mt. Pierce (Mt. Clinton)		255.3	
	57.2	Mizpah Spring Hut, Nauman Tentsite (3,800') (C,L,M,w on A.T.)	CLMw	254.5	
	58.9	Mt. Jackson		252.8	
	60.3	Mt. Webster (3,910')		251.4	
	63.5	Saco River		248.2	
N.H. Section 4	63.6	Crawford Notch, U.S. 302, Dry River Campground (1,275') (C 1.8m E; M 1m W; C,G,L 3m E; L,M 3.7m W)	RCGLM	248.1	
	66.5	Ethan Pond Shelter/Campsite (2,860')	CSw	245.2	Map 3
	71.3	Zealand Falls Hut (2,630') (L,M,w on A.T.)	LMw	240.4	

New Hampshire–Vermont

GBS	N to S	Features	Facilities (see page 8 for codes)	S to N	Map
	Miles from Maine–N.H. Line			*Miles from Vt.–Mass. Line*	
N.H. Section 4	72.5	Zeacliff		239.2	N.H.–Vt. Map 3
	75.5	Mt. Guyot, Guyot Shelter/Campsite (4,580') (C,S,w 0.8m E)	CSw	236.2	
	77.5	South Twin Mountain, North Twin Spur (4,902')		234.2	
	78.3	Galehead Hut (L,M,w on A.T.)	LMw	233.4	
	81.0	Garfield Ridge Shelter/Campsite (3,900')	CSw	230.7	
	81.4	Mt. Garfield (4,500')		230.3	
	84.9	Mt. Lafayette, Greenleaf Hut (5,260') (L,M 1.1m W; w 0.2m W)	LMw	226.8	
	85.9	Mt. Lincoln		225.8	
	86.6	Little Haystack Mountain		225.1	
	88.7	Liberty Spring Tentsite (3,870')	Cw	223.0	
N.H. Section 5	91.3	Franconia Notch, U.S. 3, Lafayette Place Campground (1,450'); **North Woodstock, N.H., P.O. 03262** (P.O.,G,L,M 5.8m E; G,L,M 2.2m E; C 2.5m W; L 1.6m E)	RCGLM	220.4	
	94.2	Lonesome Lake Hut (2,760') (L,M,w on A.T.)	LMw	217.5	
	96.1	Kinsman Pond Shelter/Campsite	CSw	215.6	
	96.7	North Kinsman Mountain		215.0	
	97.6	South Kinsman Mountain (4,358')		214.1	
	100.1	Eliza Brook Shelter/Campsite (2,400')	CSw	211.6	
	103.0	Mt. Wolf (East Peak) (3,478')		208.7	
N.H. 6	107.6	Kinsman Notch, N.H. 112 (1,870')	R	204.1	Map 4
	109.1	Beaver Brook Shelter (3,750')	Sw	202.6	
	111.4	Mt. Moosilauke (4,802')		200.3	
	116.0	Jeffers Brook Shelter (1,350')	Sw	195.7	

Appalachian Mountain Club

DOC

New Hampshire–Vermont

GBS	N to S	Features	Facilities (see page 8 for codes)	S to N	Map
	Miles from Maine–N.H. Line			*Miles from Vt.–Mass. Line*	
N.H. Section 7	117.1	N.H. 25 (1,000'); **Glencliff, N.H., P.O. 03238** (P.O.,L 0.5m E)	RL	194.6	N.H.–Vt. Map 4
	119.5	Mt. Mist (2,200')		192.2	
	122.0	N.H. 25C (1,550'); **Warren, N.H., P.O. 03279** (w on A.T.; P.O.,G,M 4m E)	RGMw	189.7	
	124.6	Ore Hill	Cw	187.1	
	125.2	Cape Moonshine Road	R	186.5	
N.H. Section 8	126.8	N.H. 25A (900'); **Wentworth, N.H., P.O. 03282** (P.O.,G,L 4.3m E)	RG	184.9	
	130.1	Side trail to Mt. Cube (North Summit) (2,911')		181.6	
	131.7	Hexacuba Shelter (w on A.T.; S 0.3m E)	Sw	180.0	
	133.1	South Jacob's Brook (1,450')	w	178.6	
	137.0	Firewarden's Cabin (3,230')	Sw	174.7	
	137.1	Smarts Mountain Tentsite	Cw	174.6	
	140.8	Lyme–Dorchester Road	Rw	170.9	N.H.–Vt. Map 5
N.H. Section 9	142.8	Dartmouth Skiway (880'); **Lyme, N.H., P.O. 03768** (P.O.,G,L,M 3.2m W)	RGLM	168.9	
	143.7	Trapper John Shelter (S,w 0.2m W)	Sw	168.0	
	144.2	Holts Ledge (1,930')		167.5	
	146.2	Goose Pond Road (952')	R	165.5	
	147.5	South Fork Hewes Brook	w	164.2	
	149.4	Moose Mountain Shelter	Sw	162.3	
	150.2	Moose Mountain (South Peak) (2,290')		161.5	
	151.8	Mink Brook	w	159.9	

Dartmouth Outing Club (DOC)

New Hampshire–Vermont

GBS	N to S	Features	Facilities (see page 8 for codes)	S to N	Map
	Miles from Maine–N.H. Line			*Miles from Vt.–Mass. Line*	
Dartmouth Outing Club (DOC) / N.H. Section 9	152.0	Three Mile Road	R	159.7	N.H.–Vt. Map 5
	154.5	Etna–Hanover Center Road (845'); **Etna, N.H., P.O. 03750** (P.O. 1.2m E)	R	157.2	
	155.9	Trescott Road	R	155.8	
	158.4	Ledyard Spring (w 0.2m W)	w	153.3	
	158.9	Velvet Rocks Shelter (S 0.2m W)	S	152.8	
	159.7	N.H. 120	R	152.0	
	160.4	Dartmouth College; **Hanover, N.H., P.O. 03755** (P.O.,G,L,M on A.T.)	☆ RGLM	151.3	
Green Mountain Club / Vt. Section 1	160.9	New Hampshire–Vermont Line, Connecticut River (400')	R	150.8	
	161.9	**Norwich, Vt., P.O. 05055** (P.O.,G,L,M 0.3m W)	☆ RGLM	149.8	
	166.2	Happy Hill Shelter/Campsite (1,460')	CSw	145.5	
	168.8	Podunk Brook, Podunk Road	Rw	142.9	
	169.6	Tigertown Road, Podunk Road	R	142.1	
Vt. Section 2	170.2	Vt. 14, White River (400'); **Hartford, Vt. P.O. 05047** (P.O. 8m E)	Rw	141.5	
	173.5	Joe Ranger Road	R	138.2	
	175.0	Thistle Hill Shelter	Sw	136.7	
	175.3	Thistle Hill (1,800')		136.4	
	177.3	Cloudland Road	R	134.4	
	179.1	Pomfret–South Pomfret Road	Rw	132.6	

New Hampshire–Vermont

GBS	N to S	Features	Facilities (see page 8 for codes)	S to N	Map
	Miles from Maine–N.H. Line			*Miles from Vt.–Mass. Line*	
Vt. 2	181.3	Woodstock Stage Road (820'); **South Pomfret, Vt., P.O. 05067** (w on A.T.; P.O.,G 0.9m E)	RGw	130.4	N.H.–Vt. Map 5
Vt. Section 3	183.5	Vt. 12 (882'); **Woodstock, Vt., P.O. 05091** (P.O.,G,L,M 4.4m E)	RGLM	128.2	
	187.3	Wintturi Shelter (1,900') (S,w 0.2m W)	Sw	124.4	N.H.–Vt. Map 6
	189.7	Side trail to The Lookout		122.0	
	192.5	Chateauguay Road	R	119.2	
	197.2	Stony Brook Shelter (1,760')	Sw	114.5	
	201.5	River Road (1,214')	R	110.2	
	202.0	Thundering Brook Road	R	109.7	
	203.2	Kent Pond (L,M,w on A.T.)	RLMw	108.5	
	203.9	Vt. 100, Gifford Woods State Park	RCSw	107.8	
	205.3	Sherburne Pass Trail (2,440')		106.4	
	206.2	Maine Junction; Junction with Long Trail; Tucker–Johnson Shelter (S 0.2m W)	S	105.5	
Vt. Section 4	207.2	U.S. 4 (1,880'); **Killington, Vt., P.O. 05751** (P.O.,G 2.2m E; L,M 0.9m E)	RGLM	104.5	
	209.1	Churchill Scott Shelter	CSw	102.6	
	211.0	Sherburne Pass Trail, Pico Camp (3,480') (S,w 0.5m E)	Sw	100.7	
	213.5	Cooper Lodge, Killington Peak Trail (3,900') (C,S,w on A.T.; M 0.2m E)	CMSw	98.2	
	217.8	Governor Clement Shelter (1,850')	Sw	93.9	
	219.4	Upper Cold River Road	Rw	92.3	

Green Mountain Club

New Hampshire–Vermont

GBS	N to S	Features	Facilities (see page 8 for codes)	S to N	Map
	Miles from Maine–N.H. Line			*Miles from Vt.–Mass. Line*	
Vt. Section 4	220.2	Gould Brook (1,480')	w	91.5	N.H.–Vt. Map 6
	221.0	Cold River Road (Lower Road)	R	90.7	
	223.0	Lottery Road	R	88.7	
	223.4	Beacon Hill		88.3	
	223.9	Clarendon Shelter	CSw	87.8	
Vt. Section 5	224.9	Vt. 103 (860'); **North Clarendon, Vt., P.O. 05759** (P.O. 4.2m W; G 0.8m W)	RG	86.8	
	225.0	Clarendon Gorge, Mill River Bridge	w	86.7	
	227.6	Minerva Hinchey Shelter (1,530')	CSw	84.1	
	231.2	Vt. 140 (1,160'); **Wallingford, Vt., P.O. 05773** (w on A.T.; P.O.,G,L,M 2.7m W; G 3.7m E)	RGLMw	80.5	
	231.3	Sugar Hill Road	R	80.4	N.H.–Vt. Map 7
	232.7	Greenwall Shelter (S,w 0.2m E)	Sw	79.0	
	233.2	Trail to White Rocks Cliff (2,400')		78.5	
	237.2	Green Mountain Trail to Homer Stone Brook Trail		74.5	
	237.4	Spring	w	74.3	
	237.5	Little Rock Pond Shelter and Tenting Area	CSw	74.2	
Vt. Section 6	239.5	Danby–Landgrove Road (USFS 10), Black Branch (1,500'); **Danby, Vt., P.O. 05739** (P.O.,G,M 3.2m W)	RGM	72.2	
	240.8	Big Branch Shelter	CSw	70.9	
	241.0	Old Job Trail to Old Job Shelter (C,S,w 1.3m E)	CSw	70.7	
	242.5	Lost Pond Shelter	CSw	69.2	

Green Mountain Club

New Hampshire–Vermont

GBS	N to S	Features	Facilities (see page 8 for codes)	S to N	Map
	Miles from Maine–N.H. Line			*Miles from Vt.–Mass. Line*	
Vt. Section 6	244.5	Baker Peak (2,850')		67.2	N.H.–Vt. Map 7
	246.5	Griffith Lake (north end)	w	65.2	
	246.7	Griffith Lake Tenting Area	Cw	65.0	
	247.2	Peru Peak Shelter	CSw	64.5	
	248.5	Peru Peak (3,429')		63.2	
	250.2	Styles Peak		61.5	
	251.8	Mad Tom Notch, USFS 21 (2,446'); **Peru, Vt., P.O. 05152** (P.O.,G 4m E; C 2.5m E)	RCGw	59.9	
	254.3	Bromley Mountain (3,260')		57.4	
	255.3	Bromley Shelter	CSw	56.4	
Vt. Section 7	257.3	Vt. 11 & 30 (1,840'); **Manchester Center, Vt., P.O. 05255** (P.O.,G,L,M 5.8m W; G 2.5m E; L,M 2.1m E)	☆ RGLM	54.4	
	259.7	Spruce Peak		52.0	
	260.1	Spruce Peak Shelter	CSw	51.6	
	262.2	Old Rootville Road, Prospect Rock	R	49.5	
	263.1	Branch Pond Trail to William B. Douglas Shelter (S,w 0.5m W)	Sw	48.6	
	265.9	Winhall River	w	45.8	
	267.8	Stratton Pond, Lye Brook Trail to Stratton View Tenting Area (2,555') (w on A.T.; C,w 0.7m W)	Cw	43.9	
	268.0	Stratton Pond Trail, Stratton Pond Shelter	Sw	43.7	
	271.0	Stratton Mountain (3,936') (G,M 1.7m E)	GM	40.7	
	274.8	Stratton–Arlington Road (Kelley Stand Road) (2,230')	Rw	36.9	

Green Mountain Club

New Hampshire–Vermont

GBS	N to S	Features	Facilities (see page 8 for codes)	S to N	Map
	Miles from Maine–N.H. Line			*Miles from Vt.–Mass. Line*	
Vt. Section 8	278.4	Story Spring Shelter	CSw	33.3	N.H.–Vt. Map 8
	279.3	South Alder Brook	w	32.4	
	283.0	Kid Gore Shelter, Caughnawaga Tentsites	CSw	28.7	
	287.0	Glastenbury Mountain (3,748')		24.7	
	287.3	Goddard Shelter	Sw	24.4	
	289.8	Glastenbury Lookout		21.9	
	291.6	Little Pond Lookout (3,060')		20.1	
	294.2	Hell Hollow Brook	w	17.5	
	295.8	Melville Nauheim Shelter	Sw	15.9	
	297.4	City Stream, Vt. 9 (1,360'); **Bennington, Vt., P.O. 05201** ☆ (P.O.,G,L,M 5m W; L 2.7m E; G 3.9m W)	RGLMw	14.3	
Vt. Section 9	299.2	Harmon Hill (2,325')		12.5	
	301.7	Congdon Shelter	CSw	10.0	
	305.9	Roaring Branch	w	5.8	
	308.6	County Road	R	3.1	
	308.9	Seth Warner Shelter and Primitive Camping Area (C,S,w 0.2m W)	CSw	2.8	
	311.3	Brook	w	0.4	
	311.7	Vermont–Massachusetts Line, southern end of Long Trail (2,330')		0.0	

Green Mountain Club

Massachusetts–Connecticut

GBS	N to S	Features	Facilities (see page 8 for codes)	S to N	Map
	Miles from Vt.-Mass. Line			*Miles from Conn.-N.Y. Line*	
Mass. Sec. 1	0.0	Vermont–Massachusetts Line, southern end of Long Trail (2,330')		140.9	Mass.–Conn. Map 1
	1.3	Pine Cobble Trail		139.6	
	2.3	Sherman Brook Primitive Campsite	Cw	138.6	
Mass. Section 2	4.1	Mass. 2 (650'); **North Adams, Mass., P.O. 01247; Williamstown, Mass., P.O. 01267** (P.O.,G,L,M 2.5m E, 2.9m W; G 2.4m E; M 0.7m E; G,M 0.5m W; L 1.6m W)	☆ RGLM	136.8	
	5.0	Pattison Road	Rw	135.9	
	7.1	Wilbur Clearing Shelter (2,300') (C,S,w 0.3m W)	CSw	133.8	
	7.2	Notch Road	R	133.7	
	10.4	Mt. Greylock, Summit Road, Bascom Lodge (3,491') (L,M,w on A.T.)	RLMw	130.5	
	10.9	Notch Road, Rockwell Road	R	130.0	
	13.1	Jones Nose Trail		127.8	
	13.7	Mark Noepel Shelter (2,800') (C,S,w 0.2m E)	CSw	127.2	
	14.6	Old Adams Road		126.3	
	17.3	Outlook Avenue	R	123.6	
Mass. Section 3	18.1	Mass. 8 (1,000'); **Cheshire, Mass., P.O. 01225** (G 0.2m W, L 0.8m E)	☆ RGL	122.8	
	18.6	Church Street, School Street (P.O.,C,M,w on A.T.)	CRMw	122.3	
	19.8	Cheshire Cobbles		121.1	
	22.3	Gore Pond (2,050')		118.6	

AMC Berkshire Chapter

Massachusetts–Connecticut

GBS	N to S	Features	Facilities (see page 8 for codes)	S to N	Map
	Miles from Vt.–Mass. Line			*Miles from Conn.–N.Y. Line*	
Mass. 3	22.7	Crystal Mountain Campsite (C,w 0.2m E)	Cw	118.2	Mass.–Conn. Map 1
	26.4	Gulf Road	R	114.5	
Mass. Section 4	27.4	Mass. 8, Mass. 9 (1,200'); **Dalton, Mass., P.O. 01226** (M on A.T.; P.O.,G,L,M 0.3m W)	☆ RL	113.5	
	28.0	CSX Railroad		112.9	
	30.1	Grange Hall Road	R	110.8	
	30.4	Kay Wood Shelter (C,S,w 0.2m E)	CSw	110.5	Mass.–Conn. Map 2
	33.1	Warner Hill (2,050')		107.8	
	33.8	Blotz Road	R	107.1	
	35.0	Cady Brook	w	105.9	
Mass. Section 5	37.0	Pittsfield Road (Washington Mountain Road); (G,L 4.6m E; M 1.8m E)	RGLM	103.9	
	38.5	West Branch Road	R	102.4	
	39.2	October Mountain Shelter (1,950')	CSw	101.7	
	41.0	County Road	R	99.9	
	43.3	Finerty Pond	w	97.6	
	45.1	Becket Mountain (2,180')		95.8	
	45.6	Tyne Road	R	95.3	
Mass. Section 6	46.4	U.S. 20 (1,400'); **Lee, Mass., P.O. 01238** (P.O.,G,L,M 5m W) (L 0.2m E)	RGLM	94.5	
	46.7	Greenwater Brook	w	94.2	
	46.8	Massachusetts Turnpike		94.1	
	48.0	Upper Goose Pond Cabin (C,S,w 0.5m W)	CSw	92.9	
	48.8	Upper Goose Pond		92.1	
	50.7	Goose Pond Road	R	90.2	

AMC Berkshire Chapter

Massachusetts–Connecticut

GBS	N to S	Features	Facilities (see page 8 for codes)	S to N	Map
	Miles from Vt.-Mass. Line			*Miles from Conn.-N.Y. Line*	
	53.1	Webster Road (1,800')	Rw	87.8	Mass.–Conn. Map 2 *AMC Berkshire Chapter*
Mass. Section 7	55.0	Tyringham Main Road (930')	R	85.9	
	56.1	Jerusalem Road	RLw	84.8	
		Tyringham, Mass., P.O. 01264 (P.O., L 0.6m W)			
	58.1	Shaker Campsite	Cw	82.8	
	58.4	Jerusalem Road (Fernside Road) (w 0.2m W)	Rw	82.5	
	61.6	Beartown Mountain Road	Rw	79.3	
	62.2	Mt. Wilcox North Shelter (2,100') (C,S,w 0.3m E)	CSw	78.7	
	63.9	Mt. Wilcox South Shelter	CSw	77.0	
	64.7	The Ledges		76.2	
	65.3	Benedict Pond (C,w 0.5m w)	RCw	75.6	
	66.1	Blue Hill Road (Stony Brook Road)	R	74.8	
Mass. Section 8	67.3	Mass. 23 (1,000');			
		Great Barrington, Mass., P.O. 01230	✫		
		(P.O.,G,L,M 4m W)	RGLM	73.6	
	68.2	Lake Buel Road (L,M 2.5m W)	RLM	72.7	
	69.3	Ice Gulch, Tom Leonard Shelter (C,S on A.T.; w 0.2m E)	CSw	71.6	
	71.4	East Mountain (1,800')	w	69.5	
	72.8	Home Road	R	68.1	
	74.8	Housatonic River	R	66.1	
	75.7	U.S. 7; **Sheffield, Mass., P.O. 01257**			
		(P.O.,G,L,M 3.3m E; M 1.0m W, 0.8m E)	RGLM	65.2	
	77.5	Sheffield–Egremont Road (700')	R	63.4	

Massachusetts–Connecticut

Chapter	GBS	N to S	Features	Facilities (see page 8 for codes)	S to N	Map
		Miles from Vt.-Mass. Line			*Miles from Conn.-N.Y. Line*	
AMC Berkshire Chapter	Mass. 9	79.3	Mass. 41 (Undermountain Road); **South Egremont, Mass., P.O. 01258** (P.O.,G,M 1.2m W)	RGM	61.6	Mass.–Conn. Map 3
	Mass. Section 10	80.2	Jug End Road (Curtiss Road) (w 0.3m E)	Rw	60.7	
		81.3	Jug End (1,750')		59.6	
		83.0	Elbow Trail		57.9	
		83.6	Glen Brook Shelter	CSw	57.3	
		83.7	The Hemlocks Shelter	Sw	57.2	
		84.1	Guilder Pond Picnic Area	R	56.8	
		84.8	Mt. Everett (2,602')		56.1	
		85.5	Race Brook Trail (C,w 0.4m E)	Cw	55.4	
		86.6	Mt. Race		54.3	
		88.5	Laurel Ridge Campsite	Cw	52.4	
AMC Connecticut Chapter	Conn. Section 1	89.7	Sages Ravine (1,340')	w	51.2	
		90.3	Sages Ravine Campsite	Cw	50.6	
		90.4	Massachusetts–Connecticut Line		50.5	
		91.5	Bear Mountain (2,316')		49.4	
		91.8	Bear Mountain Road		49.1	
		92.0	Riga Junction, Undermountain Trail		48.9	
		92.5	Brassie Brook (South Branch), Brassie Brook Shelter	CSw	48.4	
		93.1	Ball Brook Group Campsite	Cw	47.8	
		93.7	Riga Shelter	CSw	47.2	
		94.5	Lions Head (1,738')		46.4	
		96.7	Conn. 41 (Under Mountain Road); **Salisbury, Conn., P.O. 06068** (P.O.,G,L,M 0.8m W)	RGLM	44.2	
		97.4	U.S. 44 (700')	R	43.5	

Massachusetts–Connecticut

GBS	N to S	Features	Facilities (see page 8 for codes)	S to N	Map
	Miles from Vt.-Mass. Line			*Miles from Conn.-N.Y. Line*	
Conn. Section 2	100.2	Billy's View		40.7	Mass.–Conn. Map 3 *AMC Connecticut Chapter*
	101.0	Rand's View		39.9	
	101.1	Side trail to Limestone Spring Shelter (C,S,w 0.5m W)	CSw	39.8	
	101.8	Prospect Mountain (1,475')		39.1	
	103.1	Spring	w	37.8	
	103.9	Housatonic River Road	R	37.0	
	104.3	Housatonic River; **Falls Village, Conn., P.O. 06031** (P.O. 0.5m E)	R	36.6	
	106.1	Mohawk Trail (L,M 0.2m E)	LM	34.8	
	106.2	U.S. 7, Housatonic River (500')	R	34.7	
	106.8	U.S. 7, Conn. 112	R	34.1	
Conn. Section 3	107.2	Belter's Campsite	Cw	33.7	
	109.2	Hang Glider View		31.7	
	110.0	Sharon Mountain Campsite	Cw	30.9	
	111.2	Mt. Easter (1,350')		29.7	
	111.5	Mt. Easter Road	R	29.4	
	112.4	Pine Swamp Brook Shelter	CSw	28.5	
	113.5	West Cornwall Road (800'); **West Cornwall, Conn., P.O. 06796** (P.O. 2.2m E)	R	27.4	
	113.6	Carse Brook	w	27.3	
	115.8	Caesar Road, Caesar Brook Campsite	Cw	25.1	
	116.2	Pine Knob Loop Trail		24.7	
	116.9	Hatch Brook	w	24.0	
	118.1	Old Sharon Road	R	22.8	
	118.2	Guinea Brook	w	22.7	

Massachusetts–Connecticut

GBS	N to S	Features	Facilities (see page 8 for codes)	S to N	Map
	Miles from Vt.–Mass. Line			*Miles from Conn.–N.Y. Line*	
Conn. Section 4	118.3	Conn. 4; **Cornwall Bridge, Conn., P.O. 06754** (P.O.,G,L 0.9m E)	RGL	22.6	Mass.–Conn. Map 4
	119.2	Silver Hill Campsite (1,000')	C(nw)	21.7	
	120.0	River Road, Spring	Rw	20.9	
	122.0	Stony Brook Campsite	Cw	18.9	
	122.4	Stewart Hollow Brook Shelter (400')	CSw	18.5	
	124.7	River Road	R	16.2	
	125.2	St. Johns Ledges		15.7	
	125.9	Caleb's Peak (1,160')		15.0	
	126.6	Skiff Mountain Road	R	14.3	
Conn. Section 5 (N.Y. Section 1)	129.4	Conn. 341, Schaghticoke Road (350'); **Kent, Conn., P.O. 06757** (P.O.,G,L,M 0.8m E)	RGLM	11.5	
	129.7	Mt. Algo Shelter	CSw	11.2	
	130.7	Thayer Brook	w	10.2	
	132.6	Schaghticoke Mountain Campsite	Cw	8.3	
	133.2	Indian Rocks		7.7	
	133.6	Connecticut–New York Line (1,250')		7.3	
	134.8	Schaghticoke Mountain		6.1	
	136.5	Schaghticoke Road	R	4.4	
	137.2	Side trail to Bulls Bridge Road Parking Area (R 0.2m E; G,M 0.4m E)	RGM	3.7	
	137.9	Ten Mile River (280')	Cw	3.0	
	138.1	Ten Mile River Shelter	S(nw)	2.8	
	139.1	Ten Mile Hill (1,000')		1.8	
	140.2	Conn. 55	R	0.7	
	140.9	Hoyt Road, Connecticut–New York Line (400'); **Wingdale, N.Y., P.O. 12594** (P.O.,G,M 3.3m W; M 1.5m W, 2.3m W)	RGM	0.0	

AMC Connecticut Chapter

New York–New Jersey

GBS	N to S	Features	Facilities (see page 8 for codes)	S to N	Map
	Miles from Conn.–N.Y. Line			*Miles from Delaware Water Gap, Pa.*	
N.Y. Section 2	0.0	Hoyt Road, Connecticut–New York Line (400'); **Wingdale, N.Y., P.O. 12594** (P.O.,G,M 3.3m W; M 1.5m W)	RGM	162.4	N.Y.–N.J. Map 1
N.Y. Section 2	1.0	Duell Hollow Road	R	161.4	N.Y.–N.J. Map 1
N.Y. Section 2	1.2	Wiley Shelter	Sw	161.2	N.Y.–N.J. Map 1
N.Y. Section 2	1.6	Leather Hill Road (750')	R	160.8	N.Y.–N.J. Map 1
N.Y. Section 2	6.7	Hurds Corners Road	R	155.7	N.Y.–N.J. Map 1
N.Y. Section 3	6.9	N.Y. 22, Metro-North Railroad, Appalachian Trail Railroad Station (480') (G 0.6m E; L 2.6m W; M 2.4m W)	RGLM	155.5	N.Y.–N.J. Map 1
N.Y. Section 3	9.3	County 20 (West Dover Road); **Pawling, N.Y., P.O. 12564** (P.O.,G,M 3.1m W; C 3.1m E)	☆ RCGM	153.1	N.Y.–N.J. Map 1
N.Y. Section 3	10.0	Telephone Pioneers Shelter	Sw	152.4	N.Y.–N.J. Map 1
N.Y. Section 3	10.3	West Mountain (1,200')		152.1	N.Y.–N.J. Map 1
N.Y. Section 4	14.5	N.Y. 55 (720'); **Poughquag, N.Y., P.O. 12570** (P.O.,M 3.1m W; G 3.6m W; M 1.5m W; L 2.6m W)	RGLM	147.9	N.Y.–N.J. Map 1
N.Y. Section 4	14.8	Old Route 55	R	147.6	N.Y.–N.J. Map 1
N.Y. Section 4	16.7	Depot Hill Road	R	145.7	N.Y.–N.J. Map 1
N.Y. Section 4	17.8	Morgan Stewart Shelter	Sw	144.6	N.Y.–N.J. Map 1
N.Y. Section 4	17.9	Mt. Egbert (1,329')		144.5	N.Y.–N.J. Map 1
N.Y. Section 4	20.3	Stormville Mountain Road, I-84	R	142.1	N.Y.–N.J. Map 1
N.Y. 5	21.7	N.Y. 52 (800'); **Stormville, N.Y., P.O. 12582** (P.O. 1.7m W; G 2.2m W, 2.4m W; G,M 0.5m E, 2m E)	RGM	140.7	N.Y.–N.J. Map 1
N.Y. 5	23.3	Hosner Mountain Road	R	139.1	N.Y.–N.J. Map 1

New York–New Jersey Trail Conference

New York–New Jersey

GBS	N to S	Features	Facilities (see page 8 for codes)	S to N	Map
	Miles from Conn.–N.Y. Line			*Miles from Delaware Water Gap, Pa.*	
N.Y. Section 6	26.5	Taconic State Parkway	R	135.9	N.Y.–N.J. Map 1
	26.8	Hortontown Road, RPH Shelter (350')	RSw	135.6	
	28.1	Shenandoah Tenting Area	Cw	134.3	
	29.2	Long Hill Road	R	133.2	
	29.6	Shenandoah Mountain (1,282')		132.8	
N.Y. Section 7	33.8	N.Y. 301, Canopus Lake, Fahnestock State Park (C,w 1m E)	RCw	128.6	
	35.9	Sunk Mine Road (800')	R	126.5	
	37.5	Dennytown Road	RCw	124.9	
	40.2	South Highland Road	R	122.2	N.Y.–N.J. Map 2
N.Y. 8	41.2	Canopus Hill Road (420')	R	121.2	
	42.9	Old Albany Post Road, Chapman Road	R	119.5	
	43.7	Denning Hill (900')		118.7	
	45.6	Old West Point Road, Graymoor Friary	R	116.8	
N.Y. Section 9	46.2	U.S. 9, N.Y. 403 (400'); **Peekskill, N.Y., P.O. 10566** (P.O.,G,L,M 4.8m E; M 0.7m E; G on A.T.)	RGLM	116.2	
	49.6	South Mountain Pass (Manitou Road)	R	112.8	
	49.8	Hemlock Springs Campsite	Cw	112.6	
	50.8	Camp Smith Trail, Anthony's Nose (700')		111.6	
	51.5	N.Y. 9D	R	110.9	
N.Y. Section 10	52.2	Bear Mountain Bridge; **Fort Montgomery, N.Y., P.O., 10922** (P.O.,G,L,M, 0.7m W)	RGLM	110.2	
	52.3	Trailside Museum and Zoo (124')		110.1	
	53.0	Bear Mountain Inn, **Bear Mountain, N.Y., P.O. 10911** (P.O. 0.3m E; L,M,w on A.T.)	RLMw	109.4	
	54.6	Bear Mountain (1,305')	Rw	107.8	

New York–New Jersey Trail Conference

New York–New Jersey

GBS	N to S	Features	Facilities (see page 8 for codes)	S to N	Map
	Miles from Conn.–N.Y. Line			*Miles from Delaware Water Gap, Pa.*	
N.Y. Section 10	56.9	Seven Lakes Drive	R	105.5	N.Y.–N.J. Map 2
	58.7	Trail to West Mountain Shelter (S 0.6m E)	S(nw)	103.7	
	59.8	Beechy Bottom Brook	w	102.6	
	60.0	Palisades Interstate Parkway (680')	R	102.4	
	60.7	Black Mountain (1,160')		101.7	
	62.1	William Brien Memorial Shelter	S(nw)	100.3	
	63.3	Goshen Mountain		99.1	
	64.1	Seven Lakes Drive	R	98.3	
N.Y. Section 11	66.3	Arden Valley Road (1,196') (w 0.3m E)	Rw	96.1	
	67.4	Fingerboard Shelter	S(nw)	95.0	
	68.5	Surebridge Mountain		93.9	
	69.7	Lemon Squeezer		92.7	
	70.2	Island Pond Outlet	w	92.2	
	71.7	Arden Valley Road	R	90.7	
	71.8	New York State Thruway (560')		90.6	
N.Y. Section 12	72.0	N.Y. 17; **Arden, N.Y., P.O. 10910; Southfields, N.Y., P.O. 10975** (P.O. 0.7m W; P.O.,L,M 2.1m E; G 1.8m E, 5.7m E)	RGLM	90.4	
	73.2	Arden Mountain (1,180')		89.2	
	73.8	Orange Turnpike (w 0.5m E)	Rw	88.6	
	74.5	Little Dam Lake		87.9	
	75.2	East Mombasha Road	R	87.2	
	76.0	Buchanan Mountain (1,142')		86.4	
	76.9	West Mombasha Road (G 0.6m W)	RG	85.5	
	78.1	Mombasha High Point (1,280')		84.3	

New York–New Jersey Trail Conference

New York–New Jersey

GBS	N to S	Features	Facilities (see page 8 for codes)	S to N	Map
	Miles from Conn.–N.Y. Line			*Miles from Delaware Water Gap, Pa.*	
N.Y. Section 12	80.1	Fitzgerald Falls	w	82.3	N.Y.–N.J. Map 2
	80.4	Lakes Road (680')	R	82.0	
	81.9	Wildcat Shelter	Sw	80.5	
	82.2	Cat Rocks		80.2	
	82.8	Eastern Pinnacles (1,294')		79.6	
N.Y. Section 13	84.0	N.Y. 17A; **Greenwood Lake, N.Y., P.O. 10925** (G 1.6m W; P.O.,G,L,M 2m E; G,L,M 3.5m W)	RGLM	78.4	
	89.6	Prospect Rock (1,433')		72.8	N.Y.–N.J. Map 3
N.J. Section 1	90.0	State Line Trail, New York–New Jersey Line; **Hewitt, N.J., P.O. 07421** (P.O.,G,M 3.7m E)	GM	72.4	
	91.1	Long House Creek		71.3	
	92.2	Long House Road (Brady Road) (G,M 0.7m W)	RGM	70.2	
	93.6	Warwick Turnpike (1,140') (G 1.8m E, 2.7m W; L,M 0.8m W; M 1.5m E)	RGLM	68.8	
	94.1	Wawayanda Shelter (S on A.T.; w 0.4m E)	Sw	68.3	
	94.3	Wawayanda Road	R	68.1	
	94.9	Iron Mountain Road Bridge	R	67.5	
	96.0	Barrett Road; **New Milford, N.Y., P.O. 10959** (P.O.,G 1.8m W)	RG	66.4	
	97.7	Wawayanda Mountain (1,340')		64.7	

New York–New Jersey Trail Conference

New York–New Jersey

GBS	N to S	Features	Facilities (see page 8 for codes)	S to N	Map
	Miles from Conn.-N.Y. Line			Miles from Delaware Water Gap, Pa.	
N.J. Section 2	99.1	N.J. 94 (450'); **Vernon, N.J., P.O. 07462** (P.O.,G,M 2.4m E)	☆ RGM	63.3	N.Y.–N.J. Map 3
	100.0	Canal Road	R	62.4	
	100.7	Pochuck Creek footbridge		61.7	
	101.4	County 517	R	61.0	
	102.9	County 565; **Glenwood, N.J., P.O. 07418** (P.O. 0.7m W; L 1m W)	RL	59.5	
	104.1	Pochuck Mountain (800')		58.3	
	105.6	Pochuck Mountain Shelter	S(nw)	56.8	
	106.1	Lake Wallkill Road (Liberty Corners Road)	Rw	56.3	
	108.4	Wallkill River	R	54.0	
	109.4	Oil City Road	R	53.0	
N.J. Section 3	109.9	N.J. 284 (420') (G 0.4m W)	RG	52.5	
	110.9	Lott Road; **Unionville, N.Y., P.O. 10988** (P.O.,G,M 0.4m W)	RGM	51.5	
	111.8	Unionville Road	R	50.6	
	114.1	Gemmer Road	R	48.3	
	116.7	County 519	R	45.7	
	118.0	High Point Shelter	Sw	44.4	
	118.5	Side trail to High Point Monument		43.9	
N.J. Section 4	119.7	N.J. 23 (1,500') (w on A.T.; G 2.5m E, 4.3m W; L 1.4m E, 4.4m W; M 4.3m W)	RGLMw	42.7	
	122.6	Trail to Rutherford Shelter (S,w 0.4m E)	Sw	39.8	
	125.0	Deckertown Turnpike	R	37.4	
	125.2	Mashipacong Shelter	S	37.2	

New York–New Jersey Trail Conference

New York–New Jersey

GBS	N to S	Features	Facilities (see page 8 for codes)	S to N	Map
	Miles from Conn.–N.Y. Line			*Miles from Delaware Water Gap, Pa.*	
N.J. 4	127.8	Crigger Road	R	34.6	Map 3
	128.6	Sunrise Mountain (1,653')	R	33.8	
	131.0	Trail to Gren Anderson Shelter	Sw	31.4	
	132.1	Culver Fire Tower		30.3	
N.J. Section 5	134.1	Culvers Gap, U.S. 206 (935'); **Branchville, N.J., P.O. 07826** (P.O. 3.4m E; G on A.T., 1.6m E; L 2.5m E, 1.9m W; M 0.1m W, 0.6m E)	RGLM	28.3	N.Y.–N.J. Map 4
	137.7	Brink Road Shelter (S,w 0.2m W)	Sw	24.7	
	139.9	Rattlesnake Mountain (1,492')		22.5	
	141.7	Buttermilk Falls Trail		20.7	
	144.7	Blue Mountain Lakes Road	Rw	17.7	
N.J. Section 6	148.6	Millbrook–Blairstown Road (1,260')	R	13.8	
	149.0	Rattlesnake Spring	w	13.4	
	149.6	Catfish Fire Tower (1,565')		12.8	
	152.0	Camp Mohican Road, Mohican Outdoor Center (C,L,w 0.3m W)	RCLw	10.4	
	156.4	Garvey Springs Trail	w	6.0	
	156.5	Sunfish Pond (1,382')		5.9	
	157.8	Backpacker Site	C(nw)	4.6	
	159.4	Holly Spring Trail (w 0.2m E)	w	3.0	
	161.0	I-80 Overpass	R	1.4	
	161.3	Delaware Water Gap National Recreation Area Information Center	Rw	1.1	
	162.4	Delaware River Bridge (west end), New Jersey–Pennsylvania Line (350')	R	0.0	

New York–New Jersey Trail Conference

Pennsylvania

GBS	N to S	Features	Facilities (see page 8 for codes)	S to N	Map
	Miles from Delaware Water Gap, Pa.			*Miles from Pa.-Md. Line*	
Pa. Section 1	0.0	Delaware River Bridge (west end), New Jersey–Pennsylvania Line (350')	R	229.3	KTA Sections 1–6 Map; *Wilmington Trail Club*
	0.2	Pa. 611, **Delaware Water Gap, Pa., P.O. 18327** ☆ (P.O.,M 0.1m W; L,M 0.4m W; G,L 3.2m W)	RGLM	229.1	
	0.9	Council Rock		228.4	
	1.7	Lookout Rock		227.6	
	2.7	Mt. Minsi (1,461')		226.6	
	4.7	Totts Gap		224.6	
	6.6	Kirkridge Shelter (1,500')	Sw	222.7	
	7.2	Fox Gap, Pa. 191	R	222.1	*Batona*
	8.5	Wolf Rocks Bypass Trail (north end)		220.8	
	8.8	Wolf Rocks		220.5	
	9.3	Wolf Rocks Bypass Trail (south end)		220.0	
Pa. Section 2	15.7	Pa. 33 (980'); **Wind Gap, Pa., P.O. 18091** ☆ (P.O.,G,M 1m E; L 0.1m W))	RGLM	213.6	*AMC Delaware Valley Chapter*
	16.7	Hahns Lookout		212.6	
	20.3	Leroy A. Smith Shelter (S 0.1m E; w 0.2m E)	Sw	209.0	
	23.8	Smith Gap Road, Point Phillips Road (w 0.5m E)	Rw	205.5	
	24.5	Spring (w 0.6m E)	w	204.8	
	26.3	Delps Trail (1,580')		203.0	
	31.1	Little Gap (1,100'); **Danielsville, Pa., P.O. 18038** (P.O.,G,M 1.5m E; w 1.2m W)	RGMw	198.2	*Keystone Trails Assn.*
	36.2	Pa. 248	R	193.1	
	36.4	Lehigh River Bridge (east end), Pa. 873 (380'); **Palmerton, Pa., P.O. 18071** (P.O.,G,L,M 2m W)	RGLM	192.9	

Pennsylvania

GBS	N to S	Features	Facilities (see page 8 for codes)	S to N	Map
	Miles from Delaware Water Gap, Pa.			*Miles from Pa.–Md. Line*	
KTA / Pa. Section 3	36.5	Lehigh Gap, Pa. 873; **Slatington, Pa., P.O. 18080** (P.O.,G,L,M 2m E)	RGLM	192.8	KTA Sections 1–6 Map
Blue Mtn Eagle	37.1	George W. Outerbridge Shelter	Sw	192.2	
	41.5	Ashfield Road, Blue Mountain Road Lehigh Furnace Gap (1,320'); **Ashfield, Pa., P.O. 18212** (P.O.,G 2.2m W; w 0.7m E)	RGw	187.8	
	43.9	Bake Oven Knob Shelter	Sw	185.4	
Allentown Hiking Club	44.5	Bake Oven Knob (1,560')		184.8	
	44.9	Bake Oven Knob Road	R	184.4	
	46.3	Bear Rocks		183.0	
	47.0	Knife Edge		182.3	
	48.0	New Tripoli Campsite (C,w 0.2m W)	Cw	181.3	
Pa. Section 4	49.8	Pa. 309, Blue Mountain Summit (1,360') (L,M,w on A.T.)	RLMw	179.5	
	52.0	Fort Franklin Road, Blue Mountain House Road	R	177.3	
	53.9	Allentown Hiking Club Shelter	Sw	175.4	
Blue Mountain Eagle Climbing Club	55.2	Tri-County Corner (1,560')		174.1	
	61.3	Hawk Mountain Road, Eckville Shelter (600') (S,w 0.2m E)	RSw	168.0	
	66.6	The Pinnacle		162.7	
	67.0	Trail to Blue Rocks Campground (C,G,S 1.5m E)	CGS	162.3	
	68.8	Pulpit Rock (1,582')		160.5	
	70.4	Windsor Furnace Shelter (940')	Sw	158.9	
	70.6	Windsor Furnace		158.7	

Pennsylvania

GBS	N to S	Features	Facilities (see page 8 for codes)	S to N	Map
	Miles from Delaware Water Gap, Pa.			*Miles from Pa.-Md. Line*	
Pa. Map 4	73.2	Pocahontas Spring (1,200') (w on A.T.; L,M 1m E)	LMw	156.1	KTA Sections 1–6 Map
	75.8	Pa. 61 (M 0.5m W)	RM	153.5	
Pa. Section 5	76.5	**Port Clinton, Pa., P.O. 19549** (400') (P.O. on A.T.; L,S 0.5m W; G,M,L 3m E)	RGLMS	152.8	
	80.5	Phillip's Canyon Spring (1,500')	w	148.8	
	83.2	Shartlesville Cross-Mountain Road; **Shartlesville, Pa., P.O. 19554** (P.O.,G,L,M 3.6m E)	RGLM	146.1	
	85.1	Eagle's Nest Shelter (S,w 0.3m W)	Sw	144.2	
	85.8	Sand Spring Trail (w 0.2m E)	w	143.5	
	89.6	Black Swatara Spring (w 0.3m E)	w	139.7	
Pa. Section 6	90.9	Pa. 183, Rentschler Marker (1,440')	R	138.4	
	91.2	Fort Dietrich Snyder Marker (w 0.2m W)	w	138.1	
	94.5	Shuberts Gap		134.8	
	94.6	Hertlein Campsite	Cw	134.7	
	97.1	Round Head and Shower Steps	w	132.2	
	99.7	Trail to Pilger Ruh Spring	Cw	129.6	
	100.2	Pa. 501; **Pine Grove, Pa., P.O. 17963**, 501 Shelter (P.O.,M 3.7m W; S,w 0.1m W; G 4.3m W; L 5.7m W)	RGLMSw	129.1	
	102.1	Pa. 645	R	127.2	
	104.3	Blue Mountain Spring, William Penn Shelter (1,380')	Sw	125.0	

Blue Mountain Eagle Climbing Club (BMECC)

Pennsylvania

GBS	N to S	Features	Facilities (see page 8 for codes)	S to N	Map
	Miles from Delaware Water Gap, Pa.			*Miles from Pa.-Md. Line*	
BMECC; Pa. Section 7	111.2	I-81	R	118.1	KTA Sections 7–8 Map
	111.6	Swatara Gap, Pa. 72 (480') (C,G,L,M 2m E)	RGL	117.7	
	113.0	Pa. 443; Green Point, Pa.	R	116.3	
Susquehanna A. T. Club	117.7	Rausch Gap Shelter (980') (S,w 0.3m E)	Sw	111.6	
	120.0	Cold Spring Trail		109.3	
	122.3	Yellow Springs Village Site		107.0	
	125.7	Stony Mountain; Horse-Shoe Trail (1,650')		103.6	
Pa. Section 8	129.0	Pa. 325, Clarks Valley (550')	Rw	100.3	
	129.3	Spring	w	100.0	
	131.6	Shikellimy Trail		97.7	
	133.0	Kinter View (1,320')		96.3	
	134.7	Victoria Trail		94.6	
	135.7	Peters Mountain Shelter	Sw	93.6	
	136.5	Table Rock		92.8	
York HC	138.5	Pa. 225	R	90.8	
	142.4	Clarks Ferry Shelter (1,260')	Sw	86.9	
	142.6	Campsite	Cw	86.7	
	144.8	U.S. 22 & 322, Norfolk Southern Railway	R	84.5	
Mountain Club of Maryland; Pa. Section 9	145.4	Clarks Ferry Bridge (west end), Susquehanna River (380') (C on A.T.; M 0.1m W)	RCM	83.9	PATC Map 1
	145.6	Juniata River, Pa. 849	R	83.7	
	146.6	**Duncannon, Pa., P.O. 17020** (P.O.,L,M on A.T., G 0.6m W)	☆ RGLM	82.7	
	147.1	U.S. 11 & 15, Pa. 274	R	82.2	
	148.8	Hawk Rock		80.5	
	150.7	Cove Mountain Shelter (1,200')	Sw	78.6	
	155.7	Pa. 850 (650')	R	73.6	

Pennsylvania

GBS	N to S	Features	Facilities (see page 8 for codes)	S to N	Map
	Miles from Delaware Water Gap, Pa.			*Miles from Pa.-Md. Line*	
Pa. Section 10	158.0	Darlington Shelter (1,250')	Sw	71.3	MCM
	158.1	Darlington Trail, Tuscarora Trail		71.2	
	159.0	Spring	w	70.3	
	160.0	Pa. 944 (480'); Donnellytown, Pa.	R	69.3	PATC Map 1; Cumberland Valley A.T. Club
	160.9	Sherwood Drive	Rw	68.4	
	162.0	Conodoguinet Creek, Scott Farm Trail Work Center	Rw	67.3	
	163.4	I-81 Crossing	R	65.9	
	164.3	U.S. 11; **Carlisle, Pa., P.O. 17013** **New Kingston, Pa., P.O. 17072** (P.O. 5m W; 1.7m E; G 1.3m E; L,M 0.3m W; M 0.3m E)	RGLM	65.0	
	165.5	Pennsylvania Turnpike	R	63.8	
	168.2	Trindle Road (Pa. 641)	R	61.1	
	170.3	Pa. 74	R	59.0	
Pa. Section 11	172.3	Pa. 174, ATC Mid-Atlantic Regional Office; **Boiling Springs, Pa., P.O. 17007** (P.O.,w on A.T.; G,L,M 0.1m W; G 1m W)	☆ RGLMw	57.0	
	172.6	Yellow Breeches Creek (500')	R	56.7	
	172.8	Backpackers' Campsite	Cw	56.5	
	175.3	Center Point Knob (1,060')		54.0	Mountain Club of Maryland
	176.2	Alec Kennedy Shelter	Sw	53.1	
	178.3	Whiskey Spring, Whiskey Spring Road	Rw	51.0	
Pa. 12	181.1	Pa. 94 (880'); **Mount Holly Springs, Pa., P.O. 17065** (P.O.,G,M 2.5m W)	RGM	48.2	PATC 2-3
	182.9	Hunters Run Road (Pa. 34); **Gardners, Pa., P.O. 17324** (P.O. 5m E; G 0.2m E)	RG	46.4	

Pennsylvania

GBS	N to S	Features	Facilities (see page 8 for codes)	S to N	Map
	Miles from Delaware Water Gap, Pa.			*Miles from Pa.–Md. Line*	
Mountain Club of Maryland; Pa. Section 12	183.8	Pine Grove Road (C,M 0.4m W)	RCM	45.5	PATC Maps 2–3
	184.3	James Fry (Tagg Run) Shelter (S,w 0.2m E)	Sw	45.0	
	185.5	Side trail to Mountain Creek Campground (C,G 0.7m W)	CG	43.8	
	185.7	Limekiln Road	R	43.6	
	189.0	Side trail to Pole Steeple (1,300')		40.3	
Potomac A.T. Club; Pa. Section 13	191.5	Pine Grove Furnace State Park	RCGLw	37.8	
	191.8	Pa. 233 (900'), Appalachian Trail Museum	R	37.5	
	195.2	Toms Run Shelter	Sw	34.1	
	196.3	Woodrow Road	R	33.0	
	198.2	Michener Cabin (locked) (w 0.3m E)	w	31.1	
	200.1	Shippensburg Road (2,040')	R	29.2	
	201.4	Birch Run Shelter	Sw	27.9	
	203.8	Milesburn Road, Milesburn Cabin (locked)	Rw	25.5	
	204.2	Ridge Road, Means Hollow Road	R	25.1	
	204.7	Middle Ridge Road	R	24.6	
	207.3	Sandy Sod Junction (1,980')	R	22.0	
	208.8	Quarry Gap Shelters	Sw	20.5	
	209.5	Quarry Gap Road	R	19.8	
Pa. Section 14	211.4	U.S. 30, Caledonia State Park, Thaddeus Stevens Museum (960'); **Fayetteville, Pa., P.O. 17222** (P.O 3.9m W; C,w on A.T.; G 2.3m W; M 0.4m W; L 0.8mW)	RCGLMw	17.9	

Pennsylvania

GBS	N to S	Features	Facilities (see page 8 for codes)	S to N	Map
	Miles from Delaware Water Gap, Pa.			*Miles from Pa.-Md. Line*	
Pa. Section 14	214.4	Rocky Mountain Shelters (S 0.2m E; w 0.5m E)	Sw	14.9	PATC Map 4
	216.1	Pa. 233 (1,600'); **South Mountain, Pa., P.O. 17261** (P.O.,C,G,M 1.3m E)	RCGM	13.2	
	216.4	Swamp Road	R	12.9	
	219.7	Chimney Rocks (1,900')		9.6	
	221.0	Tumbling Run Shelters, Hermitage Cabin (locked)	Sw	8.3	
	221.2	Old Forge Road (1,000')	R	8.1	
	221.8	Rattlesnake Run Road	R	7.5	
	222.2	Old Forge Park	RCw	7.1	
	224.6	Deer Lick Shelters (1,420')	Sw	4.7	
	225.9	Bailey Spring	w	3.4	
	226.5	Mackie Run, Mentzer Gap Road	R	2.8	
	226.7	Pa. 16; **Blue Ridge Summit, Pa., P.O. 17214; Rouzerville, Pa., P.O. 17250; Waynesboro, Pa. P.O. 17268** ☆ (P.O.,G,M 1.3m E; P.O.,G,L,M 2.2m W, 5.7m W)	RGM	2.6	
	227.0	Old Pa. 16	R	2.3	
	228.2	Buena Vista Road	Rw	1.1	
	229.2	Pen Mar Road	R	0.1	
	229.3	Pennsylvania-Maryland Line (1,250')	R	0.0	

Potomac A.T. Club

GBS	N to S (Miles from Pa.–Md. Line)	Features	Facilities (see page 8 for codes)	S to N (Miles from Front Royal, Va.)	Map
Potomac A. T. Club / Md. Section 1	0.0	Pennsylvania–Maryland Line (1,250')	R	94.9	PATC Maps 5–6
	0.2	Pen Mar Park; **Cascade, Md., P.O. 21719** (P.O.,G,M 1.6m E; w on A.T.; M 1.4m E)	RGMw	94.7	
	3.1	Trail to High Rock	R	91.8	
	4.9	Raven Rocks Shelter (C,S 0.2m W; w 0.1m E)	CSw	90.0	
Md. Sec. 2	5.9	Raven Rock Hollow, Md. 491	R	89.0	
	6.7	Warner Gap Road	Rw	88.2	
	8.5	Foxville Road (Md. 77)	R	86.4	
	9.8	Ensign Cowall Shelter	Sw	85.1	
Md. Section 3	10.0	Wolfsville Road (Md. 17) (1,400'); **Smithsburg, Md., P.O. 21783** (P.O.,G,M 2.4m W; L 6.4m W)	RGLM	84.9	
	14.8	Pogo Memorial Campsite	Cw	80.1	
	15.4	Black Rock Cliffs (1,800')		79.5	
	16.4	Trail to Annapolis Rock (C 0.2m W; w 0.4m W)	Cw	78.5	
	18.0	Pine Knob Shelter	CSw	76.9	
Md. Section 4	18.6	I-70 Footbridge, U.S. 40 (C 1.4m W; M,w 0.5m W)	RCMw	76.3	
	19.4	Boonsboro Mountain Road	R	75.5	
	21.5	Washington Monument		73.4	
	21.9	Washington Monument Road	Rw	73.0	
	22.1	Monument Road	R	72.8	
	23.5	Turners Gap, U.S. Alt. 40 (1,000'); **Boonsboro, Md., P.O. 21713** (M on A.T; P.O.,M 2.3m W; G 1.6m W, 3.7m W)	RGM	71.4	

Maryland–West Virginia–Northern Virginia

GBS	N to S	Features	Facilities (see page 8 for codes)	S to N	Map
	Miles from Pa.–Md. Line			*Miles from Front Royal, Va.*	
Md. Section 5	23.7	Dahlgren Back Pack Campground	Cw	71.2	PATC Maps 5–6 / *Potomac A.T. Club*
	24.5	Reno Monument Road	R	70.4	
	25.5	Rocky Run Shelter (C,S,w 0.2m W)	CSw	69.4	
	27.1	Lambs Knoll (1,600')		67.8	
	27.3	White Rocks Cliff		67.6	
	27.9	Trail to Bear Spring Cabin (locked) (w 0.5m E)	w	67.0	
	30.5	Crampton Gap Shelter (C,S,w 0.3m E)	CSw	64.4	
Md. Section 6	30.9	Crampton Gap, Gathland State Park, Gapland Road (Md. 572) (950'); **Burkittsville, Md., P.O. 21718** (P.O. 1.2m E; w on A.T.)	Rw	64.0	
	32.6	Brownsville Gap		62.3	
	34.6	Ed Garvey Shelter (S on A.T.; w 0.4m E)	Sw	60.3	
	36.7	Trail to Weverton Cliffs		58.2	
Md. Section 7	37.6	Weverton Road (G 1.4m W)	RG	57.3	
	37.8	U.S. 340 Underpass		57.1	
	38.0	Keep Tryst Road (L,M 1.2m W)	RLM	56.9	
	38.1	C&O Canal Towpath (east junction)		56.8	
	39.6	U.S. 340, Sandy Hook Bridge		55.3	
	40.7	C&O Canal Towpath (west junction)		54.2	
	40.9	Potomac River, Goodloe Byron Memorial Footbridge, Maryland–West Virginia Line (250')		54.0	

Maryland–West Virginia–Northern Virginia

GBS	N to S	Features	Facilities (see page 8 for codes)	S to N	Map
	Miles from Pa.–Md. Line			*Miles from Front Royal, Va.*	
W.Va.–Va. Section 1	41.0	Shenandoah Street; Harpers Ferry National Historical Park (M 0.1m W)	RM	53.9	PATC Map 7
	41.6	Appalachian Trail Conservancy Side Trail; **Harpers Ferry, W.Va., P.O. 25425** (P.O. 0.5m W; G 1.1m W; L 0.6m W; M 0.4m W; ATC 0.2m W)	☆ RGLM	53.3	
	41.9	U.S. 340, Shenandoah River Bridge (north end) (L 0.1m W; C 1.2m W)	RCL	53.0	
	42.6	Chestnut Hill Road (W.Va. 32)	R	52.3	
	43.1	Blue Trail to Split Rock		51.8	
	43.3	West Virginia–Virginia Line (1,200')		51.6	
W.Va.–Va. Section 2	47.2	Keys Gap, W.Va. 9 (G,M,w 0.3m W, 0.3m E)	RGMw	47.7	
	50.2	David Lesser Memorial Shelter (S 0.1m E; C,w 0.3m E)	CSw	44.7	
	53.4	Trail to Blackburn Trail Center (1,650') (C 0.1m E; S,w 0.3m E)	CSw	41.5	
	54.6	Wilson Gap		40.3	
	57.5	Devils Racecourse		37.4	
	57.6	Sand Spring	w	37.3	
	58.2	Crescent Rock		36.7	
	58.3	West Virginia–Virginia Line		36.6	
	58.6	Spring	w	36.3	
	60.8	Snickers Gap, Va. 7, Va. 679 (1,000'); **Bluemont, Va., P.O. 20135** (P.O. 1.7m E; G 1m W; M 0.3m W, 0.9m W)	RGM	34.1	

Potomac A.T. Club

Maryland–West Virginia–Northern Virginia

GBS	N to S *Miles from Pa.–Md. Line*	Features	Facilities (see page 8 for codes)	S to N *Miles from Front Royal, Va.*	Map
Va. Section 3	61.4	Bears Den Rocks, Bears Den Hostel (L,w 0.2m E)	Lw	33.5	PATC Map 8 / *Potomac A.T. Club*
	64.4	Sawmill Spring, Sam Moore Shelter	Sw	30.5	
	66.4	Spring	w	28.5	
	67.6	Morgans Mill Road (Va. 605)	R	27.3	
	70.8	Fisher Loop Trail (north junction)		24.1	
	71.3	Rod Hollow Shelter	Sw	23.6	
	71.6	Fisher Loop Trail (south junction)		23.3	
Va. Section 4	74.9	Ashby Gap, U.S. 50 (900') (G,M 0.8m W; L 4m W; L,M 1.2m E)	RLM	20.0	
	77.5	Sky Meadows State Park Side Trail (C,w 1.3m E)	Cw	17.4	
	78.7	Spring	w	16.2	
	79.7	Whiskey Hollow Shelter (S,w 0.2m E)	Sw	15.2	
	82.3	Trillium Trail (1,900')		12.6	
	84.2	Manassas Gap Shelter	Sw	10.7	
Va. Section 5	86.7	Va. 55 (800'); **Linden, Va., P.O. 22642** (P.O.,G 1m W)	RG	8.2	
	88.6	Va. 638	R	6.3	
	89.7	Jim & Molly Denton Shelter	CSw	5.2	
	91.6	Mosby Campsite, Tom Sealock Spring (1,800')	Cw	3.3	
	94.9	U.S. 522 (950'); **Front Royal, Va., P.O. 22630** ☆ (P.O.,G 4.2m W; G,M 3.2m W; L,M 3.6m W)	RGLM	0.0	

Shenandoah National Park

GBS	N to S	Features	Facilities (see page 8 for codes)	S to N	Map
	Miles from Front Royal, Va.			*Miles from Rockfish Gap, Va.*	
Potomac A.T. Club — SNP Section 1 (Va. 6)	0.0	U.S. 522 (950'); **Front Royal, Va., P.O. 22630** ☆ (P.O.,G 4.2m W; G,M 3.2m W; L,M 3.6m W)	RGLM	107.8	PATC Map 9
	1.4	Va. 602	R	106.4	
	2.9	Tom Floyd Wayside	Sw	104.9	
	3.6	Possums Rest Overlook, SNP boundary; self-registration station for SNP camping permits		104.2	
	3.8	Compton Gap Horse Trail		104.0	
	5.3	Indian Run Spring (w 0.3m E)	w	102.5	
	5.6	Compton Gap; Skyline Drive, mile 10.4	R	102.2	
	6.4	Compton Peak (2,909')		101.4	
	6.8	Compton Springs	w	101.0	
	7.7	Jenkins Gap; Skyline Drive, mile 12.3	R	100.1	
	9.4	Hogwallow Gap; Skyline Drive, mile 14.2 (2,739')	R	98.4	
	10.0	Hogwallow Spring	w	97.8	
	10.9	North Marshall Mountain (3,368')		96.9	
	11.6	Skyline Drive, mile 15.9	R	96.2	
	12.1	South Marshall Mountain (3,212')		95.7	
SNP Section 2 (Va. 7)	13.2	Gravel Springs Gap; Skyline Drive, mile 17.7 (2,666')	R	94.6	
	13.4	Gravel Springs Hut (S,w 0.2m E)	Sw	94.4	
	14.5	Skyline Drive, mile 18.9	R	93.3	
	15.0	Little Hogback Mountain		92.8	
	15.1	Little Hogback Overlook; Skyline Drive, mile 19.7	R	92.7	
	15.8	First peak of Hogback		92.0	

Shenandoah National Park

GBS	N to S	Features	Facilities (see page 8 for codes)	S to N	Map
	Miles from Front Royal, Va.			*Miles from Rockfish Gap, Va.*	
SNP Section 2 (Va.7)	15.9	Spring (w 0.2m E)	w	91.9	PATC Map 9
	16.1	Second peak of Hogback (3,475')		91.7	
	16.3	Skyline Drive, mile 20.8	R	91.5	
	16.4	Third peak of Hogback		91.4	
	16.6	Skyline Drive, mile 21.1	R	91.2	
	17.0	Tuscarora Trail		90.8	
	17.6	Rattlesnake Point Overlook; Skyline Drive, mile 21.9	R	90.2	
	18.3	Range View Cabin (locked) (w 0.1m E)	w	89.5	
	19.1	Elkwallow Gap; Skyline Drive, mile 23.9 (2,480') (G,M 0.1m E)	RGM	88.7	
	19.6	Spring	w	88.2	
	24.2	Byrds Nest #4 Picnic Shelter (0.5m E)	w	83.6	
	24.3	Beahms Gap; Skyline Drive, mile 28.5	R	83.5	
	24.6	Skyline Drive, mile 28.6	R	83.2	
	25.7	Pass Mountain (3,052')		82.1	
	26.5	Pass Mountain Hut (S,w 0.2m E)	Sw	81.3	
SNP Section 3 (Va.8)	27.7	Thornton Gap, U.S. 211; Skyline Drive, mile 31.5 (2,307')	R	80.1	PATC Map 10
	29.6	Marys Rock (3,514')		78.2	
	30.2	Meadow Spring (w 0.3m E)	w	77.6	
	30.9	Byrds Nest #3 Shelter (w 0.3m E)	S	76.9	
	31.9	The Pinnacle (3,730')		75.9	

Potomac A.T. Club

Shenandoah National Park

GBS	N to S	Features	Facilities (see page 8 for codes)	S to N	Map
	Miles from Front Royal, Va.			*Miles from Rockfish Gap, Va.*	
SNP Section 3 (Va.8)	32.9	Side trail to Jewell Hollow Overlook; Skyline Drive, mile 36.4	R	74.9	PATC Map 10
	33.0	Pinnacles Picnic Ground; Skyline Drive, mile 36.7	Rw	74.8	
	35.2	Hughes River Gap; side trail to Stony Man Mountain Overlook; Skyline Drive, mile 38.6 (3,097')	Rw	72.6	
	36.8	Side trail to Stony Man summit		71.0	
SNP Section 4 (Va.9)	37.2	Skyland Service Road (north) (L,M 0.3m W)	RLM	70.6	
	38.0	Skyland Service Road (south)	R	69.8	
	40.1	Side trail to Crescent Rock Overlook; Skyline Drive, mile 44.4	R	67.7	
	40.5	Hawksbill Gap; Skyline Drive, mile 45.6 (3,361')	R	67.3	
	41.5	Side trail to Hawksbill Mountain, Byrd's Nest #2 Picnic Shelter (0.9m E)		66.3	
	41.8	Rock Spring Cabin (locked) & Hut (S,w 0.2m W)	Sw	66.0	
SNP Section 5 (Va.10)	43.7	Fishers Gap; Skyline Drive, mile 49.3	R	64.1	
	44.7	David Spring	w	63.1	
	45.3	Big Meadows (3,500') (C,L,M 0.1m E)	RCLM	62.5	
	46.2	Big Meadows Wayside, Harry F. Byrd, Sr., Visitor Center (w on A.T.; G,M 0.4m E)	RGMw	61.6	
	47.0	Spring	w	60.8	
	47.9	Milam Gap; Skyline Drive, mile 52.8	R	59.9	
	49.8	Hazeltop (3,812')		58.0	

Potomac A.T. Club

Shenandoah National Park

GBS	N to S	Features	Facilities (see page 8 for codes)	S to N	Map
	Miles from Front Royal, Va.			*Miles from Rockfish Gap, Va.*	
SNP Section 5 (Va. 10)	50.7	Bootens Gap; Skyline Drive, mile 55.1 (3,243')	R	57.1	PATC Map 10
	53.3	Bearfence Mountain Hut (S,w 0.1m E)	Sw	54.5	
	54.0	Lewis Mountain Campground; Skyline Drive, mile 57.6 (C,G,L,w 0.1m W)	RCGLw	53.8	
	55.7	Spring	w	52.1	
	56.0	Pocosin Cabin (locked)	w	51.8	
	59.3	South River Picnic Grounds (w 0.1m W)	w	48.5	
SNP Section 6 (Va. 11)	62.3	Swift Run Gap, U.S. 33; Skyline Drive, mile 65.5 (2,367')	R	45.5	PATC Map 11
	63.6	Skyline Drive, mile 66.7	R	44.2	
	65.1	Hightop Mountain (3,587')		42.7	
	65.2	Spring	w	42.6	
	65.7	Hightop Hut (S 0.1m W; w 0.2m W)	Sw	42.1	
	66.9	Smith Roach Gap; Skyline Drive, mile 68.6	R	40.9	
	68.1	Little Roundtop Mountain		39.7	
	68.5	Powell Gap; Skyline Drive, mile 69.9 (2,294')	R	39.3	
SNP Sec 7 (Va. 12)	71.8	Simmons Gap; Skyline Drive, mile 73.2	Rw	36.0	
	73.7	Pinefield Gap; Skyline Drive, mile 75.2	R	34.1	
	73.9	Pinefield Hut	Sw	33.9	
	75.5	Ivy Creek Overlook; Skyline Drive, mile 77.5	R	32.3	
	77.6	Spring (w 0.1m W)	w	30.2	

Potomac A.T. Club

Shenandoah National Park

GBS	N to S	Features	Facilities (see page 8 for codes)	S to N	Map
	Miles from Front Royal, Va.			*Miles from Rockfish Gap, Va.*	
SNP Section 7 (Va.12)	79.7	Loft Mountain Campground (3,300') (C,G,M,w 0.2m W)	CGMw	28.1	PATC Map 11
	81.8	Doyles River Cabin (locked); Skyline Drive, mile 81.1 (w 0.3m E)	Rw	26.0	
	82.7	Doyles River Parking Overlook; Skyline Drive, mile 81.9	R	25.1	
	83.1	Skyline Drive, mile 82.2	R	24.7	
SNP Section 8 (Va.13)	84.0	Browns Gap; Skyline Drive, mile 82.9 (2,600')	R	23.8	
	85.5	Skyline Drive, mile 84.3	R	22.3	
	86.5	Blackrock (3,100')		21.3	
	87.1	Blackrock Hut (S,w 0.2m E)	Sw	20.7	
	87.6	Skyline Drive, mile 87.2	R	20.2	
	87.8	Blackrock Gap; Skyline Drive, mile 87.4 (2,321')	R	20.0	
	89.6	Skyline Drive, mile 88.9	R	18.2	
	93.7	Skyline Drive, mile 92.4 (3,100')	R	14.1	
	95.7	Turk Gap; Skyline Drive, mile 94.1	R	12.1	
	97.3	Skyline Drive, mile 95.3	R	10.5	
	98.9	Spring	w	8.9	
SNP Sec 9 (Va.14)	99.1	Jarman Gap; Skyline Drive, mile 96.9; SNP southern boundary (2,173')	R	8.7	
	99.5	Spring	w	8.3	
	100.1	Calf Mountain Shelter (w 0.2m W; S 0.3m W)	Sw	7.7	
	102.3	Beagle Gap; Skyline Drive, mile 99.5	R	5.5	
	102.8	Bear Den Mountain (2,885')		5.0	
	104.1	McCormick Gap; Skyline Drive, mile 102.1	R	3.7	

Potomac A.T. Club

Shenandoah National Park

GBS	N to S	Features	Facilities (see page 8 for codes)	S to N	Map
	Miles from Front Royal, Va.			*Miles from Rockfish Gap, Va.*	
SNP Sec. 9 (Va.14)	107.0	Self-registration for SNP camping permits, park entrance station (0.2m W)		0.8	PATC Map 11 *Potomac A.T. Club*
	107.5	Skyline Drive, mile 105.2	R	0.3	
	107.7	I-64 Overpass		0.1	
	107.8	Rockfish Gap, U.S. 250, I-64 (1,902'); **Waynesboro, Va., P.O. 22980** (P.O.,G,L,M 4.5m W; G,L,M on A.T.)	☆ RGLM	0.0	

Central Virginia

GBS	N to S	Features	Facilities (see page 8 for codes)	S to N	Map
	Miles from Rockfish Gap, Va.			*Miles from New River, Va.*	
Old Dominion A.T. Club / Va. Section 15	0.0	Rockfish Gap, U.S. 250, I-64 (1,902'); **Waynesboro, Va., P.O. 22980** (P.O.,G,L,M 4.5m W)	☆ RGLM	226.8	Central Va. Map 1
	4.8	Mill Creek, Paul C. Wolfe Shelter	Sw	222.0	
	6.1	Jack Albright Trail		220.7	
	6.5	Side trail to Glass Hollow Overlook		220.3	
	7.4	Side trail to Humpback Rocks Visitors Center (w 0.5m W)	w	219.4	
	9.7	Bear Spring	w	217.1	
	10.3	Side trail to Humpback Rocks		216.5	
	11.5	Humpback Mountain (3,606')		215.3	
	14.3	Dripping Rock Parking Area; Blue Ridge Parkway, mile 9.6	Rw	212.5	
	14.8	Cedar Cliffs		212.0	
	18.6	Three Ridges Overlook; Blue Ridge Parkway, mile 13.1	R	208.2	
Tidewater A.T. Club / Va. Section 16	19.1	Reids Gap (2,645'), Va. 664; Blue Ridge Parkway, mile 13.6	R	207.7	
	20.8	Maupin Field Shelter	Sw	206.0	
	22.8	Hanging Rock Overlook		204.0	
	23.3	Three Ridges Mountain (3,970')		203.5	
	25.0	Chimney Rocks		201.8	
	27.0	Harpers Creek Shelter	Sw	199.8	
	29.7	Tye River	Cw	197.1	
NBATC / Va. Section 17	29.8	Va. 56 (997') (C,G 5m W)	RCG	197.0	
	31.1	Cripple Creek	w	195.7	
	34.1	The Priest (4,063')		192.7	
	34.6	The Priest Shelter	Sw	192.2	

Central Virginia

GBS	N to S	Features	Facilities (see page 8 for codes)	S to N	Map
	Miles from Rockfish Gap, Va.			*Miles from New River, Va.*	
Va. 17	35.5	Meadows Lane (Va. 826), Crabtree Falls Trail (C,w 0.5m W)	RCw	191.3	Central Va. Map 1
	36.3	Cash Hollow Road (3,280')	R	190.5	
	37.6	Cash Hollow Rock		189.2	
	38.4	Spy Rock		188.4	
Va. Section 18	38.9	Spy Rock Road (3,454'); **Montebello, Va., P.O. 24464** (P.O. 2.5m W; C,G,L 2.2m W)	RCGL	187.9	
	40.1	Porters Field	Cw	186.7	
	41.2	Seeley-Woodworth Shelter	Sw	185.6	
	41.9	Elk Pond Branch	Cw	184.9	
	43.1	North Fork of Piney River	Cw	183.7	
	45.0	Greasy Spring Road	R	181.8	
	45.5	USFS 246	R	181.3	
Va. Section 19	46.7	Salt Log Gap (north), USFS 63 (3,290')	R	180.1	
	48.0	Tar Jacket Ridge (3,840')		178.8	
	48.9	Hog Camp Gap, USFS 48 (3,485')	RCw	177.9	
	50.2	Cole Mountain (4,022')		176.6	
	51.4	Old Hotel Trail, Cow Camp Gap Shelter (3,428') (S,w 0.6m E)	Sw	175.4	
	52.4	Bald Knob (4,059')		174.4	
Va. Section 20	55.2	Long Mountain Wayside, U.S. 60 (2,060'); **Buena Vista, Va., P.O. 24416** (P.O.,C,G,L,M 9.3m W)	☆ RCGLM	171.6	
	57.0	Brown Mountain Creek Shelter	Sw	169.8	Map 2
	59.0	Swapping Camp Road (USFS 38)	R	167.8	
	61.9	Pedlar River Bridge	w	164.9	
	62.0	USFS 39	R	164.8	

Natural Bridge A.T. Club

Central Virginia

GBS	N to S	Features	Facilities (see page 8 for codes)	S to N	Map
	Miles from Rockfish Gap, Va.			*Miles from New River, Va.*	
Natural Bridge A.T. Club — Va. Section 21	63.9	Rice Mountain (2,169')		162.9	Central Va. Map 2
	65.8	Robinson Gap Road (Va. 607)	R	161.0	
	66.1	Blue Ridge Parkway, mile 51.7; Punchbowl Mountain Crossing (2,170')	Rw	160.7	
	66.5	Punchbowl Shelter (S,w 0.2m W)	Sw	160.3	
	67.0	Punchbowl Mountain		159.8	
	68.1	Bluff Mountain (3,391')		158.7	
	69.6	Saltlog Gap (south) (2,573')		157.2	
	70.7	Saddle Gap, Saddle Gap Trail		156.1	
	72.2	Big Rocky Row (2,974')		154.6	
	73.2	Fullers Rocks, Little Rocky Row (2,486')		153.6	
	73.3	Rocky Row Trail		153.5	
	75.3	Johns Hollow Shelter	Sw	151.5	
	75.9	Va. 812 (USFS 36)	R	150.9	
	76.0	Rocky Row Run (760')	Cw	150.8	
	76.9	Lower Rocky Row Run bridge	w	149.9	
Va. Section 22	77.0	U.S. 501, Va. 130; **Big Island, Va., P.O. 24526; Glasgow, Va., P.O. 24555** ☆ (P.O.,G,M 5.6m E; P.O.,C,G,L,M,S 5.9m W; C,G,L 4.4m E)	RCGLMS	149.8	
	77.2	James River Foot Bridge (678')		149.6	
	78.4	Campsite	Cw	148.4	
	79.2	Matts Creek Shelter	Sw	147.6	
	81.1	Big Cove Branch	w	145.7	
	81.9	Sulphur Spring Trail (north crossing) (2,588')		144.9	
	82.4	Hickory Stand, Gunter Ridge Trail		144.4	
	84.2	Sulphur Spring Trail (south crossing)		142.6	

Central Virginia

GBS	N to S	Features	Facilities (see page 8 for codes)	S to N	Map
	Miles from Rockfish Gap, Va.			*Miles from New River, Va.*	
	84.7	Marble Spring	Cw	142.1	Central Va. Map 2
	85.9	Highcock Knob (3,054')		140.9	
Va. Section 23	87.1	Petites Gap, USFS 35; Blue Ridge Parkway, mile 71.0 (2,369')	R	139.7	
	88.5	Harrison Ground Spring	w	138.3	
	90.4	Thunder Ridge Overlook; Blue Ridge Parkway, mile 74.7 (3,525')	R	136.4	
	90.8	Lower Blue Ridge Parkway crossing, mile 74.9	R	136.0	
	91.8	Thunder Hill Shelter	Sw	135.0	
	92.1	Upper Blue Ridge Parkway crossing, mile 76.3	R	134.7	
	92.7	The Guillotine		134.1	
	93.0	Apple Orchard Mountain (4,206')		133.8	
Va. Section 24	94.4	Parkers Gap Road (USFS 812); Blue Ridge Parkway, mile 78.4 (3,410')	R	132.4	
	94.5	Apple Orchard Falls Trail		132.3	
	96.2	Black Rock side trail		130.6	
	97.1	Cornelius Creek Shelter	Sw	129.7	
	97.7	Floyd Mountain (3,560')		129.1	
	102.0	Bryant Ridge Shelter (1,330')	Sw	124.8	
	104.2	Fork Mountain (2,042')		122.6	
Va. Section 25	105.8	Va. 614, Jennings Creek (987') (w on A.T.; C,G,L,M 1.6m E, L,M 4.5m W)	RCGLMw	121.0	
	107.3	Buchanan Trail		119.5	
	109.0	Cove Mountain Shelter	S(nw)	117.8	
	110.4	Little Cove Mountain Trail		116.4	
	110.8	Cove Mountain (2,707')		116.0	

Natural Bridge A.T. Club

Central Virginia

GBS	N to S	Features	Facilities (see page 8 for codes)	S to N	Map
	Miles from Rockfish Gap, Va.			*Miles from New River, Va.*	
Va. Section 26 (Natural Bridge A.T. Club)	112.4	Bearwallow Gap, Va. 43, Blue Ridge Parkway, mile 90.9 (2,228'); **Buchanan, Va., P.O. 24066** (P.O.,G,M 5m W; L,M 7m W; C,L,M 4.9m E)	RCGLM	114.4	Central Va. Map 2
	114.1	Blue Ridge Parkway, mile 91.8; Mills Gap Overlook	R	112.7	
	114.8	Blue Ridge Parkway, mile 92.5; Peaks of Otter Overlook	R	112.0	
	115.5	Bobblets Gap Shelter (S,w 0.2m W)	Sw	111.3	Central Va. Map 3
	117.9	Blue Ridge Parkway, mile 95.3; Harveys Knob Overlook	R	108.9	
	118.5	Blue Ridge Parkway, mile 95.9; Montvale Overlook	R	108.3	
	119.6	Blue Ridge Parkway, mile 97.0; Taylors Mountain Overlook	R	107.2	
Va. Section 27 (Roanoke A.T. Club)	120.4	Black Horse Gap, Old Fincastle Road (USFS 186); Blue Ridge Parkway, mile 97.7 (2,402')	R	106.4	
	122.4	Spring	w	104.4	
	122.8	Wilson Creek Shelter	Sw	104.0	
	123.5	Wilson Creek	w	103.3	
	125.4	Curry Creek	w	101.4	
	126.2	Salt Pond Road (USFS 191)	R	100.6	
	129.0	Fullhardt Knob Shelter (2,676')	Sw	97.8	
	132.0	Va. 652 (Mountain Pass Road)	R	94.8	
	132.5	Norfolk Southern Railway, U.S. 11; **Troutville, Va., P.O. 24175** (P.O.,G 0.8m W)	RG	94.3	

Central Virginia

GBS	N to S	Features	Facilities (see page 8 for codes)	S to N	Map
	Miles from Rockfish Gap, Va.			*Miles from New River, Va.*	
	132.8	Va. 779, I-81	R	94.0	
	134.0	U.S. 220; **Daleville, Va., P.O. 24083; Cloverdale, Va., P.O. 24077** (P.O. 1m W; P.O.,G,L,M 2.3m E; G,L,M on A.T.)	RGLM	92.8	
	134.5	Tinker Creek (1,165')		92.3	
	138.0	Hay Rock, Tinker Ridge		88.8	
	139.1	Angels Gap		87.7	
	143.1	Lamberts Meadow Campsite, Sawmill Run	Cw	83.7	
	143.4	Lamberts Meadow Shelter	Sw	83.4	
	144.0	Scorched Earth Gap, Andy Layne Trail		82.8	
Va. Section 28	144.5	Tinker Cliffs (3,000')		82.3	Central Va. Map 3
	146.3	Brickey's Gap		80.5	
	149.4	Campbell Shelter	Sw	77.4	
	149.5	Pig Farm Campsite	Cw	77.3	
	150.1	McAfee Knob (3,199')		76.7	
	151.4	Fire Road Connector Trail north junction		75.4	
	151.8	Catawba Mountain Shelter	Sw	75.0	
	152.8	Johns Spring Shelter	S	74.0	
	153.5	Fire Road Connector Trail south junction		73.3	
	153.8	Va. 311; **Catawba, Va., P.O. 24070** (P.O.,G 1m W; L 1.7m W; M 1.3m W)	RGLM	73.0	
	154.4	Catawba Greenway (M 1.2m W)	M	72.4	
	158.1	Va. 785 (Blacksburg Road) (1,790')	R	68.7	
	159.7	Va. 624 (Newport Road), North Mountain Trail (G 0.4m W; L 0.4m E)	RGL	67.1	
	160.7	Rawies Rest		66.1	

Roanoke A.T. Club

Central Virginia

GBS	N to S	Features	Facilities (see page 8 for codes)	S to N	Map
	Miles from Rockfish Gap, Va.			*Miles from New River, Va.*	
Va. Section 29	161.2	Lost Spectacles Gap		65.6	Cen. Va. Map 3
	162.2	Dragons Tooth, Cove Mountain (3,020')		64.6	
	166.4	Pickle Branch Shelter (S,w 0.3m E)	Sw	60.4	
	167.6	Trout Creek, Va. 620 (Miller Cove Road) (1,525')	R	59.2	
	171.4	Audie Murphy Monument (3,100')		55.4	
Va. Section 30	175.2	Craig Creek Valley, Va. 621 (1,560')	R	51.6	
	176.5	Niday Shelter	Sw	50.3	Central Va. Map 4
	177.2	Cabin Branch	Cw	49.6	
	178.9	Sinking Creek Mountain (3,490')		47.9	
	182.5	Sarver Hollow Shelter (S,w 0.4m E)	Sw	44.3	
	185.8	Va. 630, Sinking Creek (2,100')	Rw	41.0	
Va. Section 31	186.7	Sinking Creek Valley, Va. 42	R	40.1	
	187.9	Spring	w	38.9	
	189.1	Laurel Creek Shelter	Sw	37.7	
	192.1	Rocky Gap, Va. 601	R	34.7	
	193.1	Stream	w	33.7	
Va. Section 32	194.1	Johns Creek Valley, USFS 156 (2,102')	Rw	32.7	
	194.9	War Spur Shelter	Sw	31.9	
	198.6	Campsites, spring	Cw	28.2	
	199.8	Wind Rock (4,121')		27.0	
	200.0	Mountain Lake Road Salt Sulphur Turnpike (Va. 613)	R	26.8	
	203.7	Bailey Gap Shelter	S	23.1	
	203.9	Spring	w	22.9	
	205.2	Va. 635 (Big Stony Creek Road), Stony Creek (2,450')	R	21.6	
	206.2	Dismal Branch	w	20.6	

Roanoke A.T. Club (RATC)

Central Virginia

GBS	N to S	Features	Facilities (see page 8 for codes)	S to N	Map
	Miles from Rockfish Gap, Va.			*Miles from New River, Va.*	
Va. Section 33	207.3	Va. 635 (Big Stony Creek Road), Stony Creek Valley	R	19.5	Central Va. Map 4
	207.6	Pine Swamp Branch Shelter	Sw	19.2	
	210.1	Allegheny Trail		16.7	
	210.3	Peters Mountain (3,860')		16.5	
	212.5	Dickenson Gap		14.3	
	214.1	Groundhog Trail		12.7	
	215.1	Symms Gap Meadow		11.7	
	218.6	Campsite, spring	Cw	8.2	
	220.1	Rice Field Shelter (3,400')	S(nw)	6.7	
	220.7	Spring	w	6.1	
	221.7	Stream	w	5.1	
	222.9	Clendennin Road (Va. 641)	R	3.9	
	223.4	Hemlock Ridge		3.4	
	226.8	U.S. 460, Senator Shumate Bridge (east end), New River (1,600')	R	0.0	

RATC

Outdoor Club of Virginia Tech

Southwest Virginia

GBS	N to S	Features	Facilities (see page 8 for codes)	S to N	Map
	Miles from New River, Va.			*Miles from Damascus, Va.*	
Roanoke A.T. Club / Va. Section 34	0.0	U.S. 460, Senator Shumate Bridge (east end), New River (1,600')	R	166.8	SW Va. Map 1
	0.4	Va. 100, **Pearisburg, Va., P.O. 24134** (P.O.,G,L,M 1.3m E)	☆ RGLM	166.4	
	1.4	Va. 634	R	165.4	
	3.4	Angels Rest, Pearis Mountain (3,550')		163.4	
	3.9	Campsite, spring	Cw	162.9	
	9.8	Doc's Knob Shelter	Sw	157.0	
	12.1	Sugar Run Gap, Sugar Run Gap Road (Va. 663) (L 0.5m E)	RL	154.7	
	13.7	Big Horse Gap, USFS 103 (3,752')	R	153.1	
	13.8	Ribble Trail, north junction	w	153.0	
	19.3	Wapiti Shelter (2,600')	Sw	147.5	
	21.1	Stream	w	145.7	
	21.4	Ribble Trail, south junction		145.4	
	23.5	Walnut Flats Campground (C,w 0.4m W)	Cw	143.3	
	25.4	Dismal Creek Falls Trail		141.4	
Va. 35	27.3	Va. 606 (2,040') (C,G,M,w 0.5m W)	RCGMw	139.5	
	27.4	Kimberling Creek		139.4	
	29.2	Brushy Mountain (2,800')		137.6	
Va. Section 36	32.6	Va. 608, Lickskillet Hollow (2,200')	R	134.2	
	33.8	Jenny Knob Shelter	Sw	133.0	
	35.5	Brushy Mountain (3,101')		131.3	
OCVT	36.9	Va. 611	R	129.9	Map 2
	43.5	Helveys Mill Shelter (S,w 0.3m E)	Sw	123.3	
	44.9	Va. 612, Kimberling Creek	R	121.9	
	45.3	I-77 Crossing	R	121.5	

Southwest Virginia

GBS	N to S	Features	Facilities (see page 8 for codes)	S to N	Map
	Miles from New River, Va.			*Miles from Damascus, Va.*	
Va. Section 37	45.7	U.S. 52 (2,920'); **Bastian, Va., P.O. 24314; Bland, Va., P.O. 24315** (P.O. 1.8m W; P.O.,G,L,M 2.7m E)	☆ RGLM	121.1	SW Va. Map 2
	50.5	Trail Boss Trail		116.3	
	52.6	Va. 615, Laurel Creek (2,450')	RCw	114.2	
	53.4	Brushy Mountain (3,080')		113.4	
	57.0	Jenkins Shelter (2,470')	Sw	109.8	
	57.9	Stream	w	108.9	
	60.5	Davis Farm Campsite (C,w 0.4m W)	Cw	106.3	
Va. Section 38	61.5	Va. 623, Garden Mountain (3,880')	R	105.3	
	66.3	Walker Gap (3,520') (w 0.2m E)	Rw	100.5	
	67.7	Chestnut Knob Shelter (4,409')	S(nw)	99.1	
	69.5	Spring-fed pond	w	97.3	
	72.3	USFS 222 (2,300')	R	94.5	
	73.7	Lick Creek	w	93.1	
	76.0	Lynn Camp Creek (2,400')	w	90.8	
	76.6	Campsite, stream	Cw	90.2	
	77.1	Knot Maul Branch Shelter	S	89.7	
	78.3	Brushy Mountain (3,200')		88.5	
Va. Section 39	79.2	Va. 42; **Ceres, Va., P.O. 24318**	R	87.6	
	79.8	Spring	w	87.0	
	80.2	Va. 742, North Fork of Holston River		86.6	
	81.7	Va. 610	R	85.1	Map 3
	83.2	Tilson Gap, Big Walker Mountain (3,500')		83.6	
	85.1	Crawfish Valley (2,600')	Cw	81.7	
	86.2	Little Brushy Mountain (3,300')		80.6	
	89.0	Davis Path Campsite	C(nw)	77.8	
	90.1	Spring	w	76.7	

Piedmont A.T. Hikers

Southwest Virginia

GBS	N to S	Features	Facilities (see page 8 for codes)	S to N	Map
	Miles from New River, Va.			*Miles from Damascus, Va.*	
	90.8	Va. 617	R	76.0	SW Va. Map 3
Va. Section 40	91.8	Va. 683, U.S. 11, I-81 (2,420'); **Atkins, Va., P.O. 24311** (P.O. 3.1m W; G,L,M on A.T.)	RGLM	75.0	
	94.1	Va. 729	R	72.7	
	94.6	Va. 615	R	72.2	
	96.1	USFS 644	R	70.7	
	96.4	Chatfield Shelter	Sw	70.4	
	97.9	Glade Mountain (4,093')		68.9	
	99.2	USFS 86	Cw	67.6	
	99.6	Locust Mountain		67.2	
	100.6	Brushy Mountain		66.2	
	102.5	Va. 622	R	64.3	
Va. Section 41	103.2	Va. 16 (3,220'); **Sugar Grove, Va., P.O. 24375** **Marion, Va., P.O. 24354** (P.O.,G 3.1m E; P.O., G,L,M 6.6m W)	☆ RGLMw	63.6	
	103.4	Partnership Shelter	Sw	63.4	
	107.3	Va. 601	R	59.5	
	111.1	Va. 670 (Teas Road), South Fork Holston River (2,450')	R	55.7	
	112.0	Va. 672	R	54.8	
	113.2	Trimpi Shelter	Sw	53.6	
	115.3	High Point (4,040')		51.5	
	115.8	Bobby's Trail, Raccoon Branch Campground (C,w 0.2m E; 3.3m E)	Cw	51.0	
Va. 42	117.3	Dickey Gap, Va. 16, Va. 650; (*temporary detour next 2.2 miles*) **Troutdale, Va., P.O. 24378** (P.O. 2.7m E; L 2.3m E)	RL	49.5	

Piedmont A.T. Hikers / Mt. Rogers A.T. Club

Southwest Virginia

GBS	N to S	Features	Facilities (see page 8 for codes)	S to N	Map
	Miles from New River, Va.			*Miles from Damascus, Va.*	
Va. Section 42	118.5	Comers Creek, Comers Creek Falls Trail (3,200')	w	48.3	SW Va. Map 3
	118.9	Dickey Gap Trail (*temporary detour next 2.2 miles NB*) (C,w 0.4m W)	Cw	47.9	
	121.0	Stream	w	45.8	
	121.8	Hurricane Creek Trail		45.0	
	122.4	Hurricane Mountain Shelter	Sw	44.4	
	123.3	Chestnut Flats, Iron Mountain Trail		43.5	
	123.6	Hurricane Mountain (4,320'), Tennessee–New River Divide		43.2	
Va. Section 43	125.6	Va. 603, Fox Creek (3,480')	Rw	41.2	
	127.3	Old Orchard Shelter	Sw	39.5	
	128.9	Pine Mountain Trail (5,000')		37.9	
	130.3	The Scales		36.5	SW Va. Map 4
	130.7	Stone Mountain		36.1	
	133.0	Wilson Creek Trail (Cw 1.3m E)	Cw	33.8	
	133.2	Big Wilson Creek	Cw	33.6	
	133.3	Grayson Highlands State Park, Wise Shelter (4,460')	Sw	33.5	
	135.4	Park service road to Massie Gap		31.4	
	136.2	Wilburn Ridge		30.6	
	137.4	Rhododendron Gap (5,440')		29.4	
	138.4	Thomas Knob Shelter	Sw	28.4	
	138.6	Mt. Rogers Spur Trail		28.2	
	140.6	Deep Gap (w 0.2m E)	w	26.2	
	142.6	Va. 600, Elk Garden (4,434')	R	24.2	
	145.0	Whitetop Mountain Road (USFS 89)	R	21.8	
	145.1	Spring	w	21.7	

Mt. Rogers A.T. Club

Southwest Virginia

GBS	N to S	Features	Facilities (see page 8 for codes)	S to N	Map
	Miles from New River, Va.			*Miles from Damascus, Va.*	
Va. Sec. 44	145.9	Buzzard Rock (5,080'), Whitetop Mountain		20.9	SW Va. Map 4
	148.4	Va. 601 (Beech Mountain Road)	Rw	18.4	
Va. Section 45; Mt. Rogers A.T. Club	149.7	U.S. 58 (3,160'); Summit Cut, Va.	R	17.1	
	150.8	Lost Mountain Shelter	Sw	16.0	
	152.0	Va. 859 (Grassy Ridge Road)	R	14.8	
	152.6	Virginia Creeper Trail, Whitetop Laurel Creek		14.2	
	153.2	Va. 728, Creek Junction (2,720') (R 0.5m E)	R	13.6	
	155.0	Bear Tree Gap side trail (C 0.6m W)	C	11.8	
	157.3	Saunders Shelter (S,w 0.2m W)	Sw	9.5	
	157.6	Straight Mountain (3,500')		9.2	
	159.2	Taylors Valley Side Trail (M 0.6m E)	M	7.6	
	159.8	Stream	w	7.0	
	161.2	U.S. 58, Straight Branch, Feathercamp Branch (2,200'), Feathercamp Trail	Rw	5.6	
	161.8	Beech Grove Trail		5.0	
	163.3	Feathercamp Ridge, Iron Mountain Trail (2,850')		3.5	
	165.8	U.S. 58, Va. 91, Virginia Creeper Trail	R	1.0	
	166.8	**Damascus, Va., P.O. 24236** (1,928') (P.O.,G,L,M on A.T.)	☆ RGLM	0.0	

Tennessee–North Carolina

GBS	N to S	Features	Facilities (see page 8 for codes)	S to N	Map
	Miles from Damascus, Va.			*Miles from Fontana Dam, N.C.*	
Tenn.–N.C. Section 1	0.0	**Damascus, Va., P.O. 24236** (1,928') (P.O.,G,L,M on A.T.)	☆ RGLM	304.0	Tenn.–N.C. Map 1
	2.1	Campsite	Cw	301.9	
	3.7	Virginia–Tennessee Line		300.3	
	4.8	Backbone Rock Trail		299.2	
	10.2	Abingdon Gap Shelter (3,785')	CSw	293.8	
	11.3	McQueens Gap, USFS 69	R	292.7	
	11.7	McQueens Knob		292.3	
	12.7	Campsite	Cw	291.3	
	13.1	Double Spring Gap	w	290.9	
Tenn.–N.C. Section 2	15.0	Low Gap, U.S. 421 (3,384'); **Shady Valley, Tenn., P.O. 37688** (w on A.T.; P.O.,G,M 3m E)	RGMw	289.0	
	18.5	Double Springs Shelter, Holston Mountain Trail (4,080')	CSw	285.5	
	19.4	Campsite	Cw	284.6	
Tenn.–N.C. Section 3	21.5	Tenn. 91 (3,450')	R	282.5	
	22.4	Stream	w	281.6	
	24.8	Spring	w	279.2	
	24.9	Nick Grindstaff Monument		279.1	
	26.2	Iron Mountain Shelter (4,125')	CS(nw)	277.8	
	26.4	Spring	w	277.6	
	27.8	Turkeypen Gap		276.2	
	28.2	Big Laurel Branch Wilderness (north end)		275.8	
	29.2	Spring	w	274.8	
	33.0	Vandeventer Shelter (3,510') (S on A.T.; w 0.5m W)	Sw	271.0	
	34.7	Spring	w	269.3	
	37.7	Wilbur Dam Road	R	266.3	
	39.0	Watauga Dam (north end)		265.0	

MRATC | *Tennessee Eastman Hiking Club*

Tennessee–North Carolina

Tennessee Eastman Hiking Club

GBS	N to S	Features	Facilities (see page 8 for codes)	S to N	Map
	Miles from Damascus, Va.			*Miles from Fontana Dam, N.C.*	
Tenn.–N.C. 4	40.2	Stream (2,100')	w	263.8	Tenn.–N.C. Map 1
	40.6	Griffith Branch	w	263.4	
	42.1	U.S. 321; **Hampton, Tenn., P.O. 37658** (P.O.,G,M 2.6m W; G,L 1.8m W)	RGLM	261.9	
	42.6	Campsite	C	261.4	
	45.2	Pond Flats	Cw	258.8	
	48.0	Side trail to U.S. 321	w	256.0	
	48.5	Waycaster Spring	w	255.5	
	48.8	Laurel Fork Shelter (2,400')	Sw	255.2	
	49.5	Laurel Fork Falls	w	254.5	
Tenn.–N.C. Section 5	50.7	Dennis Cove, USFS 50 (C,G,L,M 0.5m E; C,L 0.2m W)	RCGLMw	253.3	Tenn.–N.C. Map 2
	52.4	Trail to Coon Den Falls		251.6	
	54.9	Campsite	Cw	249.1	
	55.8	Tower Road, White Rocks Mountain (4,206')		248.2	
	57.0	Moreland Gap Shelter	CSw	247.0	
	60.1	Campsite, stream	Cw	243.9	
	62.8	Laurel Fork	w	241.2	
	63.8	Stream	w	240.2	
	65.0	Walnut Mountain Road	R	239.0	
	65.8	Campsite	Cw	238.2	
	66.6	Mountaineer Falls Shelter	Sw	237.4	
	66.8	Mountaineer Falls Campsite	Cw	237.2	
	69.0	Sugar Hollow Campsite	Cw	235.0	
	71.8	Campbell Hollow Road	R	232.2	
	72.1	Buck Mountain Road	R	231.9	
	75.2	Bear Branch Road	R	228.8	

Tennessee–North Carolina

GBS	N to S	Features	Facilities (see page 8 for codes)	S to N	Map
	Miles from Damascus, Va.			*Miles from Fontana Dam, N.C.*	
Tenn.–N.C. Section 6	75.4	U.S. 19E (2,895'); **Roan Mountain, Tenn., P.O. 37687;** **Elk Park, N.C., P.O. 28622** (P.O.,G,M 3.4m W; P.O. 2.5m E; C 4.0m E; G 1.2m E; L 3m E; M 0.5m E, 1m E)	☆ RCGLM	228.6	Tenn.–N.C. Map 2
	76.0	Apple House Campsite	Cw	228.0	
	76.1	Wilder Mine Hollow Group Campsite	Cw	227.9	
	78.4	Doll Flats	Cw	225.6	
	80.8	Hump Mountain (5,587')		223.2	
	81.7	Bradley Gap	Cw	222.3	
	83.0	Little Hump Mountain (5,459')	Cw	221.0	
	84.6	Yellow Mountain Gap (4,682') (w 0.2m E; C 0.3m E)	Cw	219.4	
	86.5	Stan Murray Shelter (5,050')	CSw	217.5	
	88.3	Side trail to Grassy Ridge		215.7	
Tenn.–N.C. 7	90.2	Carvers Gap, Tenn. 143, N.C. 261 (5,512')	Rw	213.8	
	91.7	Roan High Knob Shelter (6,285')	Sw	212.3	
	93.8	Ash Gap	Cw	210.2	
Tenn.–N.C. Section 8	96.8	Hughes Gap (4,040') (G 3.2m W; C,L 2m E)	RCGL	207.2	
	99.0	Little Rock Knob (4,918')		205.0	
	100.2	Clyde Smith Shelter	CSw	203.8	
	101.3	Campsite	Cw	202.7	
	102.1	Greasy Creek Gap (4,034') (C,w 0.2m W; L 0.7m E)	CLw	201.9	
	105.0	Campsite	Cw	199.0	
	106.2	Iron Mountain Gap, Tenn. 107, N.C. 226 (3,723') (G 4.7m W)	RG	197.8	
	109.3	Cherry Gap Shelter	Sw	194.7	

Tennessee Eastman Hiking Club

Tennessee–North Carolina

GBS	N to S	Features	Facilities (see page 8 for codes)	S to N	Map
	Miles from Damascus, Va.			*Miles from Fontana Dam, N.C.*	
Tenn.–N.C. Section 9	110.4	Low Gap (3,900')	w	193.6	Tenn.–N.C. Map 2
	112.6	Unaka Mountain (5,180')		191.4	
	113.6	USFS 230	R	190.4	
	114.2	Beauty Spot Gap (4,100')	RCw	189.8	
	115.5	Campsite	RCw	188.5	
	115.8	Beauty Spot		188.2	
	117.0	USFS 230	R	187.0	
	118.1	Indian Grave Gap, Tenn. 395 (C 3.3m W)	RC	185.9	
	120.9	Spring	w	183.1	Tenn.–N.C. Map 3
	122.2	Curley Maple Gap Shelter (3,070')	Sw	181.8	
	125.1	Nolichucky River Valley (C,L,M on A.T.)	RCLM	178.9	
Tenn.–N.C. Section 10	126.4	Nolichucky River (1,700'); **Erwin, Tenn., P.O. 37650** (P.O.,G,M 3.8m W; L 1.2m W; G,L 2.3m W)	☆ RGLM	177.6	
	130.3	Temple Hill Gap (2,850')		173.7	
	132.7	No Business Knob Shelter	CSw	171.3	
	132.9	Spring	w	171.1	
	135.3	Devils Creek Gap (3,400')	R	168.7	
	137.0	Oglesby Branch	w	167.0	
Tenn.–N.C. Section 11	137.6	Spivey Gap, U.S. 19W (3,200')	Rw	166.4	
	138.1	Campsite	Cw	165.9	
	139.6	Trail to High Rocks (4,100')		164.4	
	139.9	Whistling Gap	Cw	164.1	
	141.9	Little Bald		162.1	
	142.9	Campsite	Cw	161.1	
	143.3	Bald Mountain Shelter	Sw	160.7	

Tennessee Eastman Hiking Club (Sections 9–10)

Carolina Mountain Club (Section 11)

Tennessee–North Carolina

GBS	N to S	Features	Facilities (see page 8 for codes)	S to N	Map
	Miles from Damascus, Va.			*Miles from Fontana Dam, N.C.*	
Tenn.–N.C. 11	144.2	Big Stamp (C,w 0.3m W; M 1.5m E)	CMw	159.8	Tenn.–N.C. Map 3 *Carolina Mountain Club*
	144.5	Big Bald (5,516')		159.5	
	145.3	Spring	w	158.7	
	147.3	Low Gap	w	156.7	
	148.7	Street Gap (4,100')		155.3	
	150.3	Springs	w	153.7	
Tenn.–N.C. Section 12	151.0	Sams Gap, U.S. 23, I-26 (3,800') (M 1.9m E, 2.8m E; G 3.2m E)	RGM	153.0	
	152.8	High Rock (4,460')		151.2	
	153.4	Hogback Ridge Shelter (C,S 0.1m E; w 0.3m E)	CSw	150.6	
	154.6	Rice Gap (3,800')		149.4	
	155.6	Big Flat	C	148.4	
	156.2	Frozen Knob (4,579')		147.8	
	159.0	Rector Laurel Road (2,960')	R	145.0	
Tenn.–N.C. Section 13	159.5	Devil Fork Gap, N.C. 212	R	144.5	
	161.3	Campsite	Cw	142.7	
	162.2	Flint Mountain Shelter (3,550')	CSw	141.8	
	163.8	Spring	w	140.2	
	167.0	Big Butt (4,750')	C	137.0	
	168.9	Jerry Cabin Shelter (4,150')	CSw	135.1	
	171.4	Big Firescald Knob	w	132.6	
	172.4	Blackstack Cliffs (0.1m W)		131.6	
	172.6	White Rock Cliffs (0.1m E		131.4	
	172.7	Spring	w	131.3	
	174.4	Camp Creek Bald, side trail to fire tower (4,750')	R	129.6	
	176.2	Little Laurel Shelter (3,300')	CSw	127.8	
	181.1	Allen Gap, N.C. 208, Tenn. 70 (2,234')	Rw	122.9	

Tennessee–North Carolina

Carolina Mountain Club

GBS	N to S	Features	Facilities (see page 8 for codes)	S to N	Map
	Miles from Damascus, Va.			*Miles from Fontana Dam, N.C.*	
Tenn.–N.C. Sec. 14	183.3	Spring	w	120.7	Tenn.–N.C. Map 4
	184.8	Spring Mountain Shelter (3,300')	CSw	119.2	
	186.5	Hurricane Gap	R	117.5	
	187.6	Rich Mountain Fire Tower Side Trail (3,600')	Cw	116.4	
	189.9	Tanyard Gap, U.S. 25 & 70 (2,278')	R	114.1	
	192.5	Pump Gap		111.5	
	194.4	Lovers Leap Rock		109.6	
Tenn.–N.C. Section 15	195.8	U.S. 25 & 70, N.C. 209 (1,326'); **Hot Springs, N.C., P.O. 28743** (P.O.,C,G,L,M on A.T.)	☆ RCGLM	108.2	
	199.0	Deer Park Mountain Shelter	CSw	105.0	
	202.4	Garenflo Gap (2,500')	R	101.6	
	204.9	Big Rock Spring	w	99.1	
	206.5	Bluff Mountain (4,686')		97.5	
	208.9	Walnut Mountain Shelter (C 0.1m W)	CSw	95.1	
	210.2	Lemon Gap, N.C. 1182, Tenn. 107 (3,550')	R	93.8	
	213.7	Roaring Fork Shelter	CSw	90.3	
	215.6	Max Patch Summit (4,629')		88.4	
Tenn.–N.C. Section 16	216.4	Max Patch Road (N.C. 1182)	R	87.6	
	219.1	Brown Gap	Rw	84.9	
	222.0	Deep Gap, Groundhog Creek Shelter (2,900') (C,S,w 0.2m E)	CSw	82.0	
	224.0	Campsite	Cw	80.0	
	224.5	Snowbird Mountain (4,263')	R	79.5	
	226.0	Spanish Oak Gap		78.0	
	226.9	Painter Branch	Cw	77.1	
	229.2	Green Corner Road (C,G,L 0.2m W)	RCGL	74.8	

Tennessee–North Carolina

GBS	N to S	Features	Facilities (see page 8 for codes)	S to N	Map
	Miles from Damascus, Va.			*Miles from Fontana Dam, N.C.*	
	229.7	I-40	R	74.3	
	230.1	Pigeon River (1,400')		73.9	
	230.3	State Line Branch	Cw	73.7	
	231.6	Davenport Gap, Tenn. 32, S.R. 1397; eastern boundary, Great Smoky Mountains National Park (1,975') (C 2.5m E)	RC	72.4	
	232.7	Davenport Gap Shelter	Sw	71.3	
	234.9	Spring	w	69.1	
	236.4	Spring	w	67.6	
	236.8	Mt. Cammerer Side Trail (5,000')		67.2	
	238.9	Low Gap Trail		65.1	
	239.6	Cosby Knob Shelter	Sw	64.4	
	240.0	Cosby Knob		64.0	
	243.3	Snake Den Ridge Trail		60.7	
	245.3	Guyot Spring	w	58.7	
	245.9	Guyot Spur (6,360')		58.1	
	247.3	Tri-Corner Knob Shelter	Sw	56.7	
	248.4	Mt. Chapman		55.6	
	250.1	Mt. Sequoyah		53.9	
	252.5	Pecks Corner Shelter (w on A.T.; S,w 0.5m E)	Sw	51.5	
	254.5	Bradleys View		49.5	
	257.6	Porters Gap, The Sawteeth		46.4	
	259.0	Charlies Bunion		45.0	
	259.9	Icewater Spring Shelter	Sw	44.1	
	260.2	Boulevard Trail to Mt. LeConte		43.8	
	263.0	Newfound Gap, U.S. 441 (5,045')	Rw	41.0	
	264.7	Indian Gap	R	39.3	
	266.1	Spring	w	37.9	

GBS: Tenn.–N.C. Section 17 (N.C. 1)

Map: Tenn.–N.C. Map 4; Great Smoky Mtns. N.P. Map

CMC / *Smoky Mountains Hiking Club*

Tennessee–North Carolina

GBS	N to S	Features	Facilities (see page 8 for codes)	S to N	Map
	Miles from Damascus, Va.			*Miles from Fontana Dam, N.C.*	
Smoky Mountains Hiking Club; Tenn.–N.C. Section 18 (N.C. 2)	267.9	Mt. Collins Shelter (5,900') (S,w 0.5m W)	Sw	36.1	Great Smoky Mtns. N.P. Map
	270.2	Mt. Love		33.8	
	270.7	Clingmans Dome (6,643') (R,w 0.5m E)	Rw	33.3	
	273.5	Double Spring Gap Shelter (5,507')	Sw	30.5	
	275.0	Silers Bald		29.0	
	275.2	Silers Bald Shelter	Sw	28.8	
	278.2	Buckeye Gap (4,817'), Miry Ridge Trail	w	25.8	
	280.6	Sams Gap, Greenbrier Ridge Trail	w	23.4	
	280.9	Derrick Knob Shelter	Sw	23.1	
	281.9	Sugar Tree Gap (4,435')		22.1	
	283.6	Mineral Gap (5,030')		20.4	
	284.2	Beechnut Gap	w	19.8	
	285.3	Thunderhead, east peak (5,527')		18.7	
	285.9	Rocky Top		18.1	
	287.0	Eagle Creek Trail to Spence Field Shelter, Bote Mountain Trail (S,w 0.2m E)	Sw	17.0	
	289.9	Russell Field Shelter	Sw	14.1	
	291.4	Little Abrams Gap (4,120')		12.6	
	292.5	Devils Tater Patch (4,775')		11.5	
	293.0	Mollies Ridge Shelter	Sw	11.0	
	294.7	Ekaneetlee Gap (3,842')	w	9.3	
	296.2	Doe Knob (4,520')		7.8	
	298.4	Birch Spring Gap	Cw	5.6	
	299.7	Shuckstack fire tower (0.1m E)		4.3	
	304.0	Little Tennessee River, Fontana Dam; southern boundary, Great Smoky Mountains National Park (1,800')	R	0.0	

North Carolina–Georgia

GBS	N to S	Features	Facilities (see page 8 for codes)	S to N	Map
	Miles from Fontana Dam, N.C.			*Miles from Springer Mountain, Ga.*	
N.C. Section 3	0.0	Little Tennessee River, Fontana Dam; southern boundary, Great Smoky Mountains National Park (1,740')	R	166.7	N.C.–Ga. Map 1
	0.4	Fontana Dam Visitor Center	Rw	166.3	
	0.8	Fontana Dam Shelter	CSw	165.9	
	2.0	N.C. 28; **Fontana Dam, N.C., P.O. 28733** (P.O.,G,L,M 1.8m W)	☆ RGLM	164.7	
	4.3	Campsite	Cw	162.4	
	4.7	Walker Gap (3,450')		162.0	
	6.1	Black Gum Gap		160.6	
	7.5	Cable Gap Shelter	CSw	159.2	
N.C. Section 4	8.4	Yellow Creek Gap, S.R. 1242 (2,980') (Yellow Creek Mountain Road) (L 4m E)	RL	158.3	
	10.8	Cody Gap	Cw	155.9	
	11.6	Hogback Gap		155.1	
	13.4	Brown Fork Gap	w	153.3	
	13.8	Brown Fork Gap Shelter	Sw	152.9	
	15.2	Sweetwater Gap		151.5	
N.C. Section 5	16.2	Stecoah Gap, N.C. 143 (3,165') (Sweetwater Creek Road)	Rw	150.5	
	18.3	Simp Gap		148.4	
	19.3	Locust Cove Gap	Cw	147.4	
	21.7	Cheoah Bald (5,062')		145.0	
	22.9	Sassafras Gap Shelter	CSw	143.8	
	23.8	Swim Bald		142.9	
	26.9	Grassy Gap (3,050')		139.8	
	28.4	Wright Gap	R	138.3	

Smoky Mountains Hiking Club

North Carolina–Georgia

GBS	N to S	Features	Facilities (see page 8 for codes)	S to N	Map
	Miles from Fontana Dam, N.C.			*Miles from Springer Mountain, Ga.*	
N.C. Section 6	30.0	U.S. 19, U.S. 74, Nantahala River (1,723'); Trail of Tears; Wesser, N.C. (L,M on A.T.; G 1m E)	RGLM	136.7	N.C.–Ga. Map 2
	30.8	A. Rufus Morgan Shelter	CSw	135.9	
	33.9	Jump-up Lookout (4,000')		132.8	
	35.7	Wesser Creek Trail, Wesser Bald Shelter	CS	131.0	
	35.8	Spring	w	130.9	
	36.5	Wesser Bald (4,627'), viewing tower (0.1m E)		130.2	
N.C. Section 7	37.9	Tellico Gap, S.R. 1365 (3,850')	R	128.8	
	39.3	Big Branch Campsite	Cw	127.4	
	39.6	Side trail to Rocky Bald Lookout		127.1	
	40.8	Copper Ridge Bald Lookout (5,080')		125.9	
	41.5	Cold Spring Shelter	CSw	125.2	
	42.7	Burningtown Gap, S.R. 1397 (4,236')	R	124.0	
	45.0	Licklog Gap (C 0.1 W, w 0.3m W)	Cw	121.7	
	46.3	Wayah Shelter	CSw	120.4	
	46.8	Campsite	Cw	119.9	
	47.2	Wayah Bald (5,342')	R	119.5	
	49.1	Wine Spring	Cw	117.6	
	49.6	USFS 69	Rw	117.1	
N.C. Section 8	51.4	Wayah Gap, S.R. 1310 (4,180')	R	115.3	
	53.1	Siler Bald Shelter (4,700') (C,S,w 0.5m E)	CSw	113.6	
	55.3	Panther Gap		111.4	
	56.2	Swinging Lick Gap		110.5	
	56.4	Moore Creek Campsite	Cw	110.3	

Nantahala Hiking Club

North Carolina–Georgia

GBS	N to S	Features	Facilities (see page 8 for codes)	S to N	Map
	Miles from Fontana Dam, N.C.			*Miles from Springer Mountain, Ga.*	
N.C. 8	57.3	Winding Stair Gap, U.S. 64; **Franklin, N.C., P.O. 28734** (w on A.T.; P.O.,G,L,M 10m E)	☆ RGLMw	109.4	N.C.–Ga. Map 2
N.C. Section 9	60.4	Wallace Gap, “Old 64” (3,738')	R	106.3	
	61.0	Rock Gap, Standing Indian Campground (C 1.5m W)	RC	105.7	
	61.1	Rock Gap Shelter	CSw	105.6	
	63.6	Glassmine Gap		103.1	
	64.5	Long Branch Shelter	CSw	102.2	
	67.0	Albert Mountain (5,250')		99.7	
	67.3	Bearpen Trail, USFS 67	R	99.4	
	68.3	Spring	w	98.4	
	68.6	Mooney Gap, USFS 83	R	98.1	
	69.5	Betty Creek Gap (4,300')	Cw	97.2	
	73.2	Carter Gap Shelter	CSw	93.5	
	73.6	Timber Ridge Trail		93.1	
	76.4	Beech Gap (4,460')	Cw	90.3	
	79.3	Lower Ridge Trail, Standing Indian Mountain (5,498') (w 0.2m W)	w	87.4	
	80.8	Standing Indian Shelter	CSw	85.9	
N.C. Section 10	81.7	Deep Gap, USFS 71 (4,341') (C 0.1m W)	CRw	85.0	
	83.8	Wateroak Gap		82.9	
	84.7	Chunky Gal Trail		82.0	
	84.9	Whiteoak Stamp	Cw	81.8	
	85.7	Muskrat Creek Shelter (4,600')	CSw	81.0	
	86.6	Sassafras Gap		80.1	
	88.5	Bly Gap (3,840')	Cw	78.2	
	88.6	North Carolina–Georgia Line		78.1	
	90.5	Rich Cove Gap		76.2	

Nantahala Hiking Club

North Carolina–Georgia

GBS	N to S	Features	Facilities (see page 8 for codes)	S to N	Map
	Miles from Fontana Dam, N.C.			*Miles from Springer Mountain, Ga.*	
Ga. Section 11	90.7	Spring	w	76.0	N.C.–Ga. Map 3
	91.7	Blue Ridge Gap (3,020')		75.0	
	92.3	As Knob		74.4	
	93.0	Plumorchard Gap Shelter (C,S,w 0.2m E)	CSw	73.7	
	94.2	Bull Gap (3,550')		72.5	
	95.7	Cowart Gap		71.0	
	96.4	Little Bald Knob Campsite	Cw	70.3	
Ga. Section 12	97.5	Dicks Creek Gap, U.S. 76 (2,675'); **Hiawassee, Ga., P.O. 30546** (w on A.T.; L 3.5m W; P.O.,G,L,M 11m W)	☆ RGLMw	69.2	
	98.1	Streams	w	68.6	
	98.7	Moreland Gap		68.0	
	99.7	Powell Mountain (3,850')		67.0	
	99.9	McClure Gap	C	66.8	
	101.1	Deep Gap Shelter (3,550') (C,S,w 0.3m E)	CSw	65.6	
	101.9	Kelly Knob (4,276')		64.8	
	102.9	Addis Gap (3,304') (C,w 0.5m E)	Cw	63.8	
	103.8	Sassafras Gap	w	62.9	
	104.9	Swag of the Blue Ridge		61.8	
	108.5	Tray Mountain Shelter (C,S 0.2m W; w 0.3m W)	CSw	58.2	
	109.0	Tray Mountain (4,430')		57.7	
	109.8	Tray Gap, Tray Mountain Road (USFS 79/698)	R	56.9	
	110.5	Cheese Factory Site	Cw	56.2	
	110.8	Tray Mountain Road (USFS 79)	R	55.9	

Georgia A.T. Club

North Carolina–Georgia

GBS	N to S	Features	Facilities (see page 8 for codes)	S to N	Map
	Miles from Fontana Dam, N.C.			*Miles from Springer Mountain, Ga.*	
Ga. Sec. 12	111.5	Indian Grave Gap, USFS 283 (3,113')	R	55.2	N.C.–Ga. Map 3; *Georgia A.T. Club*
	112.8	Rocky Mountain (4,017')	C	53.9	
	113.6	Stream	w	53.1	
	114.2	Unicoi Gap, Ga. 75 (2,949'); **Helen, Ga., P.O. 30545** (P.O.,G,L,M 9m E; C,G,L,M 3.8m W)	☆ RCGLM	52.5	
Ga. Section 13	115.7	Blue Mountain (4,025')		51.0	
	116.6	Blue Mountain Shelter	CSw	50.1	
	117.3	Spring	w	49.4	
	117.5	Spaniards Knob Campsite	C	49.2	
	118.2	Red Clay Gap		48.5	
	118.9	Chattahoochee Gap (3,500')	w	47.8	
	120.1	Cold Springs Gap		46.6	
	122.5	Poplar Stamp Gap	Cw	44.2	
	123.9	Low Gap Shelter (3,050')	CSw	42.8	
	124.7	Sheep Rock Top		42.0	
	126.5	Poor Mountain		40.2	
	127.6	White Oak Stamp		39.1	
	128.5	Hogpen Gap, Ga. 348 (3,450')	Rw	38.2	
	128.7	Whitley Gap Shelter (S 1.2m E; w 1.5m E)	Sw	38.0	
Ga. Section 14	129.4	Tesnatee Gap, Ga. 348 (3,138')	R	37.3	
	130.4	Cowrock Mountain (3,842')		36.3	
	131.2	Baggs Creek Gap	Cw	35.5	
	131.7	Wolf Laurel Top		35.0	
	132.4	Rock Spring Top	w	34.3	
	133.2	Swaim Gap		33.5	
	133.9	Levelland Mountain (3,942')		32.8	
	134.3	Bull Gap	Cw	32.4	

North Carolina–Georgia

GBS	N to S	Features	Facilities (see page 8 for codes)	S to N	Map
	Miles from Fontana Dam, N.C.			*Miles from Springer Mountain, Ga.*	
Georgia A.T. Club; Ga. Section 15	135.4	Neel Gap, U.S. 19/129 (3,125') (G,L on A.T.; L 0.3m E; C,G 3m W; C,L 3.5m W)	☆ RCGLw	31.3	N.C.–Ga. Map 4
	136.4	Flatrock Gap, Trail to Byron Reece Memorial (w 0.2m W)	w	30.3	
	137.8	Blood Mountain Shelter (4,461')	S(nw)	28.9	
	138.6	Slaughter Creek Campsites	Cw	28.1	
	138.7	Slaughter Creek Trail	w	28.0	
	139.0	Bird Gap (3,650'), Woods Hole Shelter (S,w 0.5m W)	CSw	27.7	
	140.4	Jarrard Gap (3,250') (w 0.3m W; w 1m W, G,L 2m W)	GLw	26.3	
	141.0	Burnett Field Mountain		25.7	
	142.7	Lance Creek Campsite	Cw	24.0	
	143.8	Dan Gap		22.9	
	144.8	Big Cedar Mountain (3,737')		21.9	
Ga. Section 16	146.2	Woody Gap, Ga. 60 (3,173'); **Suches, Ga., P.O. 30572** (w 0.1m W; P.O.,C,G 2m W)	☆ RCGw	20.5	
	147.7	Ramrock Mountain		19.0	
	149.8	Gooch Gap, USFS 42 (2,821')	Rw	16.9	
	151.0	Gooch Mountain Shelter (C,S,w 0.1m W)	CSw	15.7	
	152.5	Justus Creek (2,550')	Cw	14.2	
	154.5	Cooper Gap, USFS 42/80	R	12.2	
	156.2	Horse Gap (2,673')	R	10.5	
	158.1	Hightower Gap, USFS 42/69 (2,854')	R	8.6	
	158.6	Hawk Mountain Shelter (S 0.2m W; w 0.4m W)	Sw	8.1	
	159.3	Hawk Mountain Campsite	Cw	7.4	

North Carolina–Georgia

GBS	N to S	Features	Facilities (see page 8 for codes)	S to N	Map
	Miles from Fontana Dam, N.C.			*Miles from Springer Mountain, Ga.*	
Ga. Section 17	160.5	USFS 251	R	6.2	N.C.–Ga. Map 4 *Georgia A.T. Club*
	161.5	Side trail to Long Creek Falls, junction with Benton MacKaye and Duncan Ridge trails		5.2	
	162.4	Three Forks, USFS 58 (2,530')	RCw	4.3	
	162.5	Benton MacKaye Trail		4.2	
	162.9	Stover Creek	w	3.8	
	163.8	Stover Creek	w	2.9	
	163.9	Stover Creek Shelter (C,S,w 0.2m E)	CSw	2.8	
	164.8	Benton MacKaye Trail		1.9	
	165.7	USFS 42	R	1.0	
	166.4	Southern terminus, Benton MacKaye Trail		0.3	
	166.5	Springer Mountain Shelter (C,S,w 0.2m E)	CSw	0.2	
	166.7	Springer Mountain (3,782')		0.0	

Amicalola Falls Approach Trail

GBS	N to S	Features	Facilities (see page 8 for codes)	S to N	Map
Georgia A.T. Club — Approach Trail	*Miles from Springer Mountain, Ga.*			*Miles from Amicalola Falls State Park*	N.C.–Ga. Map 4
	0.0	Springer Mountain (3,782')		8.8	
	1.5	Black Gap Shelter	CSw	7.3	
	2.8	Nimblewill Gap, USFS 28 (3,100')	R	6.0	
	3.4	Side trail to Len Foote Hike Inn (L,M,w 1m E)	LMw	5.4	
	3.7	Frosty Mountain Road (USFS 46)	R	5.1	
	4.0	Frosty Mountain (3,382')	Cw	4.8	
	5.6	High Shoals Road	R	3.2	
	7.3	USFS 46	R	1.5	
	7.4	Side trail to Len Foote Hike Inn (L,M,w 5m E)	LMw	1.4	
	7.6	Amicalola Lodge Road (L,M,w 0.2m E)	RLMw	1.2	
	8.8	Visitors Center, Amicalola Falls State Park (1,700')	RCSw	0.0	

A.T. Maintaining Clubs

Maine A.T. Club	www.matc.org
Appalachian Mountain Club	www.outdoors.org
Randolph Mountain Club	www.randolphmountainclub.org
Dartmouth Outing Club	outdoors.dartmouth.edu
Green Mountain Club	www.greenmountainclub.org
AMC Berkshire Chapter	www.amcberkshire.org
AMC Connecticut Chapter	www.ct-amc.org
New York–New Jersey Trail Conference	www.nynjtc.org
Wilmington Trail Club	www.wilmingtontrailclub.org
Batona Hiking Club	batona.wildapricot.org
AMC Delaware Valley Chapter	www.amcdv.org
Keystone Trails Association	www.kta-hike.org
Blue Mountain Eagle Climbing Club	www.bmecc.org
Allentown Hiking Club	www.allentownhikingclub.org
Susquehanna A.T. Club	www.satc-hike.org
York Hiking Club	www.yorkhikingclub.com
Cumberland Valley A.T. Club	www.cvatclub.org
Mountain Club of Maryland	www.mcomd.org
Potomac A.T. Club	www.patc.net
Old Dominion A.T. Club	www.odatc.net
Tidewater A.T. Club	www.tidewateratc.org
Natural Bridge A.T. Club	www.nbatc.org
Roanoke A.T. Club	www.ratc.org
Outdoor Club of Virginia Tech	www.outdoor.org.vt.edu
Piedmont A.T. Hikers	www.path-at.org
Mount Rogers A.T. Club	www.mratc.org
Tennessee Eastman Hiking Club	www.tehcc.org
Carolina Mountain Club	www.carolinamountainclub.org
Smoky Mountains Hiking Club	www.smhclub.org
Nantahala Hiking Club	www.nantahalahikingclub.org
Georgia A.T. Club	www.georgia-atclub.org

History of the *Appalachian Trail Data Book*

The model for the *Appalachian Trail Data Book* was the "Mileage Fact Sheet" compiled by Ed Garvey and Gus Crews, published simultaneously in 1971 by the Appalachian Trail Conference and Appalachian Books (Oakton, Va.) as an appendix to the late Mr. Garvey's *Appalachian Hiker.*

The first edition (1977) of the *Appalachian Trail Data Book* was compiled by the late Raymond F. Hunt of Kingsport, Tenn., who continued to perform this volunteer service annually until 1983, when he began a six-year term as chair of the ATC.

The editions since then have been compiled by another volunteer, Daniel D. Chazin of Teaneck, N.J., an active volunteer with the New York–New Jersey Trail Conference and editor of the *Appalachian Trail Guide to New York–New Jersey.* Mr. Chazin draws each fall on the work of editors and data compilers of the other 10 guidebooks, more than 30 maintaining clubs, and Conservancy regional offices for information on the various sections of the Appalachian Trail.

The Appalachian Trail Community Network

The Appalachian Trail Community program is an ATC initiative that seeks to develop mutually beneficial relationships with interested towns and counties along the Trail—to enhance their economies, further protect the Trail, and engage a new generation of volunteers.

Communities designated as of November 2020 were:

Millinocket, Maine
Monson, Maine
Kingfield, Maine
Rangeley, Maine
Gorham, New Hampshire
Hanover, New Hampshire
Norwich, Vermont
Manchester, Vermont
Bennington, Vermont
North Adams, Massachusetts
Cheshire, Massachusetts
Dalton, Massachusetts
Great Barrington, Massachusetts
Harlem Valley (Dover and Pawling), New York
Warwick, New York
Vernon, New Jersey
Greater Blairstown, New Jersey
Delaware Water Gap, Pennsylvania
Wind Gap, Pennsylvania
Duncannon, Pennsylvania
Boiling Springs, Pennsylvania
Greater Waynesboro, Pennsylvania
Harpers Ferry/Bolivar, West Virginia
Round Hill, Virginia
Berryville/Clarke County, Virginia
Front Royal/Warren County, Virginia
Luray/Page County, Virginia
Harrisonburg, Virginia
Nelson County, Virginia
Waynesboro, Virginia
Buena Vista, Virginia
Glasgow, Virginia
Troutville, Virginia
Narrows, Virginia
Pearisburg, Virginia
Bland, Virginia
Marion/Smyth County, Virginia
Abingdon, Virginia
Damascus, Virginia
Roan Mountain, Tennessee
Erwin/Unicoi County, Tennessee
Hot Springs, North Carolina
Fontana Dam, North Carolina
Franklin, North Carolina
Hiawassee/Towns County, Georgia
Helen/White County, Georgia
Union County (Blairsville, Suches), Georgia
Dahlonega, Georgia
Ellijay/Gilmer County, Georgia

Those listed in the *Data Book* are indicated by a ☆ in the Facilities column.

Protect, enhance, and promote the Trail experience: That's what we do.

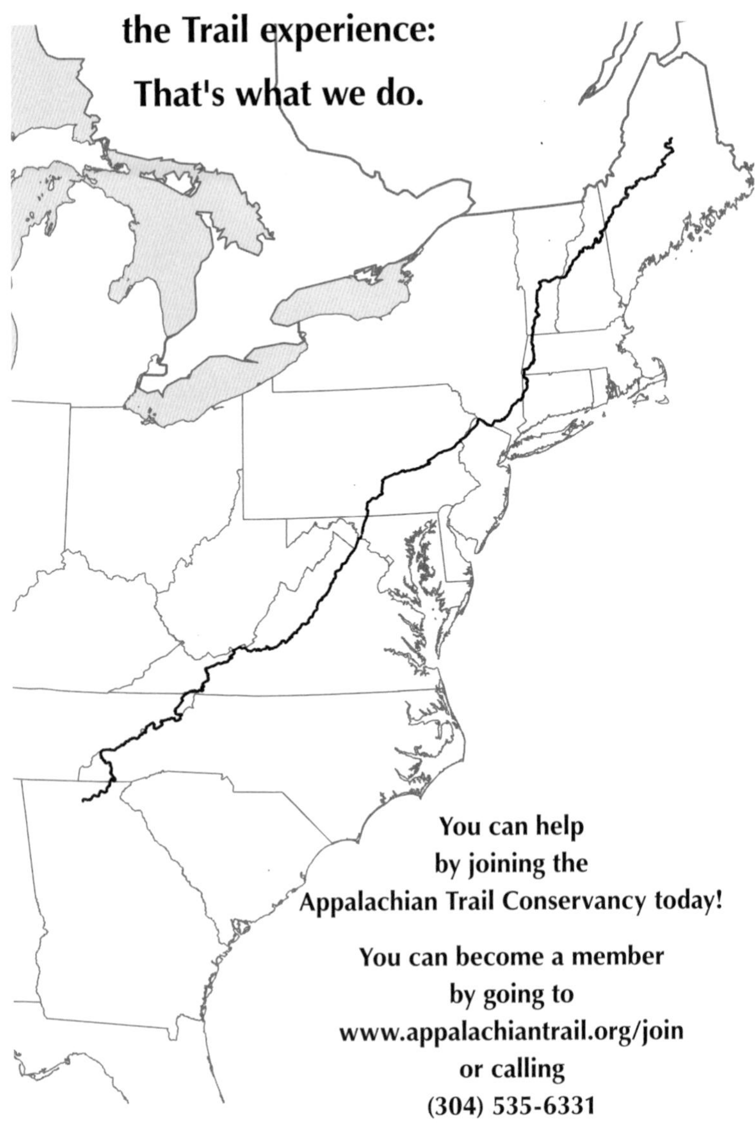

You can help
by joining the
Appalachian Trail Conservancy today!

You can become a member
by going to
www.appalachiantrail.org/join
or calling
(304) 535-6331